QUICK AND EASY
CHINESE
KITCHEN

QUICK AND EASY
CHINESE
KITCHEN

FAST, HEALTHY COOKING
WITH EXOTIC INGREDIENTS

Linda Doeser

HERMES
HOUSE

First published in 1998 by Hermes House

© Anness Publishing Limited 1998

Hermes House is an imprint of Anness Publishing Limited
Hermes House, 88–89 Blackfriars Road, London SE1 8HA

ISBN 1 84038 188 4

A CIP catalogue record for this book is available from the British Library

Publisher: Joanna Lorenz
Project Editor: Linda Doeser
Copy Editor: Harriette Lanzer
Designers: Ian Sandom, Siân Keogh

Photography: Karl Adamson, Edward Allwright, David Armstrong,
Steve Baxter, James Duncan, Michelle Garrett, Amanda Heywood, Patrick McLeavey,
Michael Michaels, Thomas Odulate
Styling: Madeleine Brehaut, Michelle Garrett, Maria Kelly, Blake Minton, Kirsty Rawlings
Food for Photography: Carla Capalbo, Kit Chan, Elizabeth Wolf-Cohen, Joanne Craig,
Nicola Fowler, Carole Handslip, Jane Hartshorn, Shehzad Husain, Wendy Lee,
Lucy McKelvie, Annie Nichols, Jane Stevenson, Steven Wheeler
Illustrations: Madeleine David

Front Cover: Lisa Tai, Designer; Tom Odulate, Photographer;
Helen Trent, Stylist; Lucy McKelvie, Home Economist

Previously published as part of a larger compendium, *The Ultimate Chinese & Asian Cookbook*

Printed in Hong Kong/China

1 3 5 7 9 10 8 6 4 2

NOTES
For all recipes, quantities are given in both metric and imperial measures and,
where appropriate, in standard cups and spoons. Follow one set, but not a mixture,
because they are not interchangeable.

Standard spoon and cup measurements are level.
1 tsp = 5ml, 1 tbsp = 15ml; 1 cup = 250ml/8fl oz

Australian standard tablespoons are 20ml. Australian readers should use 3 tsp in place of
1 tbsp for measuring small quantities of gelatine, cornflour, salt, etc.

Medium eggs should be used unless otherwise stated.

CONTENTS

INTRODUCTION

Chinese food has become increasingly popular in the West during the last three decades, moving gradually from restaurants to home kitchens. Part of its charm, for the cook at least, is the speed at which it can be prepared. Delicious, aromatic and unusual meals can be ready in minutes. Moreover, because the food is cooked so rapidly it keeps many of its vitamins, its colour and texture.

❦

The wok and stir-frying reign supreme in the Chinese kitchen. This round-based pan is designed to cook finely sliced or chopped ingredients rapidly and evenly. The food must be kept on the move throughout cooking, but it takes only a little practice to perfect the technique. But Chinese cooking is not all stir-frying – steaming, poaching, deep-frying and baking all play important roles, too.

❦

This book begins with a useful glossary of some more unfamiliar ingredients, spices and sauces. This is followed by advice on equipment and a basic guide to stir-frying, deep-frying and steaming in a wok. The recipes are divided into six chapters: Soups & Appetizers, Fish & Seafood, Meat & Poultry, Vegetables, Noodles & Rice, and Desserts. All the recipes are superbly illustrated in colour with easy-to-follow step-by-step instructions. Hints and tips throughout offer helpful suggestions and variations of the recipes.

❦

From Corn and Crab Meat Soup to Toffee Apples, all the dishes can be cooked in 15 minutes and many of them take even less time.

INGREDIENTS

Bamboo shoots Mild-flavoured, tender shoots of the young bamboo, widely available fresh, or sliced or halved in cans.

Basil Several different types of basil are used in Asian cooking. Thai cooks use two varieties, holy and sweet basil, but ordinary basil works well.

Bean curd See under Tofu.

Beansprouts Shoots of the mung bean, usually available from supermarkets. They add a crisp texture to stir-fries.

Black bean sauce Made of salted black beans crushed and mixed with flour and spices (such as ginger, garlic or chilli) to form a thickish paste. It is sold in jars or cans and, once opened, should be kept in the refrigerator.

Cardamom pods Available both as small green pods and larger black pods containing seeds, they have a strong aromatic quality.

Cashew nuts Whole cashew nuts feature prominently in Chinese stir-fries, especially those with chicken.

Cassia bark A form of cinnamon, but with a more robust flavour.

Chilli bean sauce Made from fermented bean paste mixed with hot chilli and other seasonings. Sold in jars, some chilli bean sauces are quite mild, but some are very hot. You will have to try out the various brands yourself to see which one is to your taste.

Chilli oil Made from dried red chillies, garlic, onions, salt and vegetable oil, this is used more as a dip than as a cooking ingredient.

Chilli sauce A very hot sauce made from chillies, vinegar, sugar and salt. Usually sold in bottles, it should be used sparingly in cooking or as a dip. Tabasco sauce can be a substitute.

Chillies There is a wide range of fresh and dried chillies from which to choose. Generally the larger the chilli, the milder the flavour, but there are some exceptions, and the only way to gauge potency is by taste. Remove the seeds for a milder flavour. Whether using dried or fresh chillies, take care when preparing them as their seeds and flesh can "burn": wash your hands immediately afterwards or, better still, wear rubber gloves – and never rub your eyes.

Chinese cabbage Also known as Chinese leaves, two sorts are widely available. The most commonly seen variety has a pale green colour and tightly wrapped elongated head, and about two-thirds of the cabbage is stem which has a crunchy texture. The other type has a shorter and fatter head with curlier, pale yellow or green leaves, and white stems.

Chinese chives Better known as garlic chives, these are sometimes sold with their flowers.

Chinese five-spice powder This flavouring contains star anise, pepper, fennel, cloves and cinnamon.

Chinese pancakes Thin flour and water pancakes with no added seasonings or spices. They are available fresh or frozen.

Chinese rice wine Made from glutinous rice, this is also known as yellow wine – *huang jin* or *chiew* – because of its colour. The best variety is called Shao Hsing or Shaoxing and comes from the south-east of China. Dry sherry may be used as a substitute.

Coconut milk and cream Coconut milk should not be confused with the "milk" or juice found inside a fresh coconut (though the latter makes a refreshing drink). The coconut milk used for cooking is produced from the white flesh of the nut. If left to stand, the thick part of the milk will rise to the surface like cream.

To make your own, break open a fresh coconut and remove the brown inner skin from the flesh. Grate sufficient flesh to measure 400ml/14 fl oz/1⅔ cups. Place the grated flesh, together with 300ml/½ pint/1¼ cups water, in a blender or food processor fitted with a metal blade and process for 1 minute. Strain the mixture through a sieve lined with muslin into a bowl. Gather up the corners of the muslin and squeeze out the liquid. The coconut milk is then ready to use, but you should stir it before use.

Coconut milk is also available in cans, as a soluble powder and as creamed coconut which is sold in block form. Powder and creamed coconut make a poor milk, but are useful for sauces and dressings.

Coriander Fresh coriander has a strong, pungent smell that combines well with other rich flavours. The white coriander root is used when the green colouring is not required. The seeds are also used, whole and ground.

Cornflour paste To make cornflour paste, mix 4 parts cornflour with about 5 parts cold water until smooth.

Cumin Available as whole seeds and as a powder, cumin has a strong, slightly bitter flavour and is used mainly in Indian recipes, and also in many Asian dishes.

Curry paste Curry paste is traditionally made by pounding fresh herbs and spices in a mortar with a pestle. The two types of Thai curry paste, red and green, are made with red and green chillies respectively. Other ingredients vary with individual cooks, but red curry paste typically contains ginger, shallots, garlic, coriander and cumin seeds and lime juice, as well as chillies. Herbs and flavourings in green curry paste usually include spring onions, fresh coriander, kaffir lime leaves, ginger, garlic and lemon grass. Making curry paste is time-consuming, but it tastes excellent and keeps well. Ready-made pastes, available in packets and tubs, are satisfactory substitutes.

Top shelf, left to right: *garlic, ginger, lemon grass, dried shrimps, Thai fish sauce, Szechuan peppercorns, sweet chilli sauce, ground coriander, galangal, Chinese five-spice powder, fresh green chillies*
Middle shelf: *dried red chillies, peanuts (skins on), cardamom pods, cashew nuts (in jar), peanuts (skins off), kaffir lime leaves, tamarind, hoisin sauce, salted black beans, chilli oil*
Bottom shelf, back row: *sake, rice vinegar, Chinese rice wine*
Bottom shelf, middle row: *sesame oil, mirin, peanut oil, fresh coriander, cumin seeds*
Bottom shelf, front row: *basil, dried shrimp paste, red and green chillies, flaked coconut and creamed coconut, light soy sauce, oyster sauce, pieces of coconut, whole coconut*

Lemon grass Also known as citronella, lemon grass has a long, pale green stalk and a bulbous end similar to that of a spring onion. Only the bottom 13cm/5in are used. It has a woody texture and an aromatic, lemony scent. Unless finely chopped, it is always removed before serving because it is so fibrous.

Dashi Light Japanese stock, available in powder form. The flavour derives from kelp seaweed. Diluted vegetable stock made from a cube may be substituted.

Dried shrimps and shrimp paste Dried shrimps are tiny shrimps that are salted and dried. They are used as a seasoning for stir-fried dishes. Soak them first in warm water until soft, then either process them in a blender or food processor or pound them in a mortar with a pestle. Shrimp paste, also known as *terasi*, is a dark, odorous paste made from fermented shrimps. Use sparingly.

Fish sauce The most commonly used flavouring in Thai food. Fish sauce (*nam pla*) is used in Thai cooking in the same way as soy sauce is used in Chinese dishes. It is made from salted anchovies and has a strong, salty flavour.

Galangal Fresh galangal, also known as *lengkuas*, tastes and looks a little like ginger with a pinkish tinge to its skin. Prepare it in the same way. It is also available dried and ground.

Garlic Garlic, together with ginger, is an indispensable ingredient in Chinese and Asian cooking.

Ginger Fresh ginger root has a sharp, distinctive flavour. Choose firm, plump pieces of fresh root with unwrinkled, shiny skins.

Gram flour Made from ground chick-peas, this flour has a unique flavour and is worth seeking out in Indian food stores.

Hoisin sauce A thick, dark brownish-red sauce which is sweet and spicy.

Kaffir lime leaves These are used rather like bay leaves, but to give an aromatic lime flavour to dishes. The fresh leaves are available from oriental food stores and can be frozen for future use.

Lengkuas See under Galangal.

Mirin A mild, sweet, Japanese rice wine used in cooking.

Miso A fermented bean paste that adds richness and flavour to Japanese soups.

Mooli A member of the radish family with a fresh, slightly peppery taste and white skin and flesh. Unlike other radishes, it is good when cooked, but should be salted and allowed to drain first, as it has a high water content. It is widely used in Chinese cooking and may be carved into an elaborate garnish.

Mushrooms Chinese shiitake mushrooms are used both fresh and dried to add texture and flavour to a dish. Wood ears are used in their dried form. All dried mushrooms need to be soaked in warm water for 20–30 minutes before use. Dried mushrooms are expensive, but a small quantity goes a long way.

Noodles: Cellophane noodles, also known as bean thread, transparent or glass noodles, are made from ground mung beans. Dried noodles must be soaked in hot water before cooking.

Egg noodles are made from wheat flour, egg and water. The dough is flattened and then shredded or extruded through a pasta machine to the required shape and thickness.

Rice noodles are made from ground rice and water. They range in thickness from very thin to wide ribbons and sheets. Dried ribbon rice noodles are usually sold tied together in bundles. Fresh rice noodles are also available. Rinse rice noodles in warm water and drain before use.

Rice vermicelli are thin, brittle noodles that look like white hair and are sold in large bundles. They cook almost instantly in hot liquid, provided the noodles are first soaked in warm water. They can also be deep-fried.

Somen noodles are delicate, thin, white Japanese noodles made from wheat flour in dried form, usually tied in bundles held together with a paper band.

Udon noodles, also Japanese, are made of wheat flour and water. They are usually round, but can also be flat and are available fresh, precooked or dried.

Nori Paper-thin sheets of Japanese seaweed.

Oyster sauce Made from oyster extract, this is used in many Asian fish dishes, soups and sauces.

Pak choi Also known as bok choi, this is a leaf vegetable with long, smooth, milky white stems and dark green foliage.

Palm sugar Strongly flavoured, hard brown sugar made from the sap of the coconut palm tree. It is available in oriental stores. If you have trouble finding it, use soft dark brown sugar instead.

Peanut oil This oil can be heated to a high temperature, making it perfect for stir-frying and deep-frying.

Peanuts Used in wok cookery to add flavour and a crunchy texture. The thin red skins must be removed before cooking, by immersing the peanuts in boiling water for a few minutes and then rubbing off the skins.

Red bean paste A reddish-brown paste made from puréed red beans and crystallized sugar. It is sold in cans.

Rice Long-grain rice is generally used for savoury dishes. There are many high-quality varieties, coming from a range of countries. Basmati, which means fragrant in Hindi, is generally acknowledged as the king of rices. Thai jasmine rice is also fragrant and slightly sticky.

Rice vinegar There are two basic types of rice vinegar: red vinegar is made from fermented rice and has a distinctive dark colour and depth of flavour; white vinegar is stronger in flavour as it is distilled from rice. If rice vinegar is unavailable, cider vinegar may be substituted.

Sake A strong, powerful, fortified rice wine from Japan.

Dried noodles

1 ribbon noodles, 2 somen noodles,
3 udon noodles, 4 soba noodles,
5 egg ribbon noodles, 6 medium egg noodles,
7 cellophane noodles, 8 rice sheets,
9 rice vermicelli, 10 egg noodles,
11 rice ribbon noodles

Sesame oil This is used more for flavouring than for cooking. It is very intensely flavoured, so only a little is required.

Soy sauce A major seasoning ingredient in Asian cooking, this is made from fermented soy beans combined with yeast, salt and sugar. Chinese soy sauce falls into two main categories: light and dark. Light soy sauce has more flavour than the sweeter dark soy sauce, which gives food a rich, reddish colour.

Spring roll wrappers Paper-thin wrappers made from wheat or rice flour and water. Wheat wrappers are usually sold frozen and should be thawed and separated before use. Rice flour wrappers are dry and must be soaked before use.

Sweet potato The sweet richness of this red tuber marries well with the hot-and-sour flavours of South-east Asia. In Japan the sweet potato is used to make delicious candies and sweetmeats.

Szechuan peppercorns Also known as farchiew, these aromatic, red peppercorns are best used roasted and ground. They are not so hot as either white or black peppercorns, but do add a unique taste.

Tamarind The brown, sticky pulp of the bean-like seed pod of the tamarind tree. It is used in Thai and Indonesian cooking to add tartness to recipes, rather as western cooks use vinegar or lemon juice. It is usually sold dried or pulped. The pulp is diluted with water and strained before use. Soak 25g/1oz tamarind pulp in 150ml/¼ pint/⅔ cup warm water for about 10 minutes. Squeeze out as much tamarind juice as possible by pressing all the liquid through a sieve.

Terasi See under Dried Shrimps and Shrimp Paste.

Tofu This custard-like preparation of puréed and pressed soya beans, also known as bean curd, is high in protein. Plain tofu is bland in flavour but readily absorbs the flavours of the food with which it is cooked. Tofu is also available

smoked and marinated. Firm blocks of tofu are best suited to stir-frying.

Turmeric A member of the ginger family, turmeric is a rich, golden-coloured root. If you are using the fresh root, wear rubber gloves when peeling it to avoid staining your skin. Turmeric is also available in powder form.

Wasabi This is an edible root, which is used in Japanese cooking to make a condiment with a sharp, pungent and fiery flavour. It is very similar to horseradish and is available fresh, and in powder and paste form.

Water chestnuts Walnut-sized bulbs from an Asian water plant that look like sweet chestnuts. They are sold fresh by some oriental food stores, but are more readily available canned.

Wonton wrappers Small, paper-thin squares of wheat-flour and egg dough.

Top shelf, left to right: *fresh egg noodles, wonton wrappers, water chestnuts, cellophane noodles, gram flour, spring roll wrappers*
Middle shelf: *dried Chinese mushrooms, pak choi, tofu, dried egg noodles, Chinese pancakes*
Bottom shelf, at back: *rice; (in basket) mangetouts, baby sweetcorn, shallots, shiitake mushrooms; Chinese cabbage, rice vermicelli*
Bottom shelf, at front: *bamboo shoots, beansprouts, wood ears (mushrooms), spring onions, yard-long beans*

Yard-long beans Long, thin beans similar to French beans but three or four times longer. Cut into smaller lengths and use just like ordinary green beans.

Yellow bean sauce A thick paste made from salted, fermented yellow soya beans, crushed with flour and sugar.

EQUIPMENT

You don't need specialist equipment to produce a Chinese or Asian meal – you can even use a heavy-based frying pan instead of a wok in many instances. However, the items listed below will make your oriental dishes easier and more pleasant to prepare.

Wok There are many different varieties of wok available. All are bowl-shaped with gently sloping sides that allow the heat to spread rapidly and evenly over the surface. One that is about 35cm/14in in diameter is a useful size for most families, allowing adequate room for deep-frying, steaming and braising, as well as stir-frying.

Originally always made from cast iron, woks are now manufactured in a number of different metals. Cast iron remains very popular as it is an excellent conductor of heat and develops a patina over a period of time that makes it virtually non-stick. Carbon steel is also a good choice, but stainless steel tends to scorch. Non-stick woks are available but are not really very efficient because they cannot withstand the high heat required for wok cooking. They are also expensive.

Woks may have an ear-shaped handle or two made from metal or wood, a single long handle or both. Wooden handles are safer.

Seasoning the wok New woks, apart from those with a non-stick lining, must be seasoned. Many need to be scrubbed first with a cream cleanser to remove the manufacturer's protective coating of oil. Once the oil has been removed, place the wok over a low heat and add about 30ml/2 tbsp vegetable oil. Rub the oil over the entire inside surface of the wok with a pad of kitchen paper. Heat the wok slowly for 10–15 minutes, then wipe off the oil with more kitchen paper. The paper will become black. Repeat this process of coating, heating and wiping several times until the paper is clean. Once the wok has been seasoned, it should not be scrubbed again. After use, just wash it in hot water without using any detergent, then wipe it completely dry before storage.

Wok accessories There is a range of accessories available to go with woks, but they are by no means essential.

Lid This is a useful addition, particularly if you want to use the wok for steaming and braising, as well as frying. Usually made of aluminium, it is a close-fitting, dome-shaped cover. Some woks are sold already supplied with matching lids. However, any snug-fitting, dome-shaped saucepan lid is an adequate substitute.

Stand This provides a secure base for the wok when it is used for steaming, braising or deep-frying and is a particularly useful accessory. Stands are always made of metal but vary in form, usually either a simple open-sided frame or a solid metal ring with holes punched around the sides.

Trivet This is essential for steaming to support the plate above the water level. Trivets are made of wood or metal.

Scoop This is a long, often wooden-handled, metal spatula with a wooden end used to toss ingredients during stir-frying. Any good, long-handled spoon can be used instead, although it does not have quite the same action.

Bamboo steamer This fits inside the wok where it should rest safely perched on the sloping sides. Bamboo steamers range in size from small for dumplings and dim sum to those large enough to hold a whole fish.

Bamboo strainer This wide, flat, metal strainer with a long bamboo handle makes lifting foods from steam or hot oil easier. A slotted metal spoon can also be used.

Other equipment Most equipment required for cooking the recipes in this book will be found in any kitchen. However, specialist tools are generally simple and inexpensive, especially if you seek out authentic implements from oriental stores.

A selection of cooking utensils, clockwise from top: bamboo steamer, pestle and mortar, chopping board with cleaver, chef's knife and small paring knife, wok with lid and draining wire, wok scoop

Cleaver No Chinese cook would be without one. This is an all-purpose cutting tool, available in various weights and sizes. It is easy to use and serves many purposes from chopping up bones to precision cutting, such as deveining prawns. It is a superb instrument for slicing vegetables thinly. It must be kept very sharp.

Pestle and mortar Usually made of earthenware or stone, this is extremely useful for grinding small amounts of spices and for pounding ingredients together to make pastes.

Food processor This is a quick and easy alternative to the pestle and mortar for grinding spices and making pastes. It can also be used for chopping and slicing vegetables.

COOKING TECHNIQUES

STIR-FRYING

This quick technique retains the fresh flavour, colour and texture of ingredients, and its success depends upon having all that you require ready prepared before starting to cook.

1 Heat an empty wok over a high heat. This prevents food sticking and will ensure an even heat. Add the oil and swirl it around so that it coats the base and half-way up the sides of the wok. It is important that the oil is hot when the food is added, so that it will start to cook immediately.

2 Add the ingredients in the order specified in the recipe. Aromatics (garlic, ginger, spring onions) are usually added first: do not wait for the oil to get so hot that it is almost smoking or they will burn and become bitter. Toss them in the oil for a few seconds. Next add the main ingredients that require longer cooking, such as dense vegetables or meat. Follow with the faster-cooking items. Toss the ingredients from the centre of the wok to the sides using a wok scoop, long-handled spoon or wooden spatula.

DEEP-FRYING

A wok is ideal for deep-frying as it uses far less oil than a deep-fat fryer. Make sure that it is fully secure on its stand before adding the oil and never leave the wok unattended.

1 Put the wok on a stand and half-fill with oil. Heat until the required temperature registers on a thermometer. Alternatively, test it by dropping in a small piece of food: if bubbles form all over the surface of the food, the oil is ready.

2 Carefully add the food to the oil, using long wooden chopsticks or tongs, and move it around to prevent it sticking. Use a bamboo strainer or slotted spoon to remove the food. Drain on kitchen paper before serving.

STEAMING

Steamed foods are cooked by a gentle moist heat, which must circulate freely in order for the food to cook. Steaming is increasingly popular with health-conscious cooks as it preserves flavour and nutrients. It is perfect for vegetables, meat, poultry and especially fish. The easiest way to steam food in a wok is using a bamboo steamer.

USING A BAMBOO STEAMER

1 Put the wok on a stand. Pour in sufficient boiling water to come about 5cm/2in up the sides and bring back to simmering point. Carefully put the bamboo steamer into the wok so that it rests securely against the sloping sides without touching the surface of the water.

2 Cover the steamer with its matching lid and cook for the time recommended in the recipe. Check the water level from time to time and top up with boiling water if necessary.

USING A WOK AS A STEAMER

Put a trivet in the wok, then place the wok securely on its stand. Pour in sufficient boiling water to come just below the trivet. Carefully place a plate containing the food to be steamed on the trivet. Cover the wok with its lid, bring the water back to the boil, then lower the heat so that it is simmering gently. Steam for the time recommended in the recipe. Check the water level from time to time and top up with boiling water if necessary.

SOUPS &
APPETIZERS

Chinese Tofu and Lettuce Soup

This light, clear soup is brimful of nourishing, tasty vegetables.

INGREDIENTS

Serves 4

30ml/2 tbsp groundnut or
 sunflower oil
200g/7oz smoked or marinated
 tofu, cubed
3 spring onions, sliced diagonally
2 garlic cloves, cut in thin strips
1 carrot, thinly sliced in rounds
1 litre/1¾ pints/4 cups vegetable stock
30ml/2 tbsp soy sauce
15ml/1 tbsp dry sherry or vermouth
5ml/1 tsp sugar
115g/4oz Cos lettuce, shredded
salt and ground black pepper

1 Heat the oil in a preheated wok, then stir-fry the tofu cubes until browned. Drain and set aside on kitchen paper.

2 Add the onions, garlic and carrot to the wok and stir-fry for 2 minutes. Pour in the stock, soy sauce, dry sherry or vermouth, sugar and lettuce. Heat through gently for 1 minute, season to taste and serve hot.

Crab and Egg Noodle Broth

This delicious broth is the ideal solution when you are hungry, time is short and you need a fast, nutritious and filling meal.

INGREDIENTS

Serves 4

75g/3oz thin egg noodles
25g/1oz/2 tbsp unsalted butter
1 small bunch spring onions, chopped
1 celery stick, sliced
1 medium carrot, cut into batons
1.2 litres/2 pints/5 cups chicken stock
60ml/4 tbsp dry sherry
115g/4oz white crab meat, fresh or
    frozen
pinch of celery salt
pinch of cayenne pepper
10ml/2 tsp lemon juice
1 small bunch coriander or flat-leaf
    parsley, roughly chopped, to garnish

1 Bring a large saucepan of salted water to the boil. Toss in the egg noodles and cook according to the instructions on the packet. Cool under cold running water and leave immersed in water until required.

COOK'S TIP

Fresh and frozen crab meat have a better flavour than canned crab, which tends to taste rather bland.

2 Heat the butter in another large pan, add the spring onions, celery and carrot, cover and cook the vegetables over a gentle heat for 3-4 minutes until soft.

3 Add the chicken stock and dry sherry, bring to the boil and simmer for a further 5 minutes.

4 Flake the crab meat between your fingers on to a plate and remove any stray pieces of shell.

5 Drain the noodles and add to the broth together with the crab meat. Season to taste with celery salt and cayenne pepper and stir in the lemon juice. Return to a simmer.

6 Ladle the broth into shallow soup plates, scatter with roughly chopped coriander or parsley and serve immediately.

Corn and Crab Meat Soup

Surprisingly, this soup originated in the United States, but it has since been introduced into mainstream Chinese cookery. It is important that you make sure you use creamed sweetcorn in the recipe to achieve exactly the right consistency.

INGREDIENTS

Serves 4

115g/4oz crab meat or chicken
   breast fillet
2.5ml/½ tsp finely chopped root ginger
2 egg whites
30ml/2 tbsp milk
15ml/1 tbsp cornflour paste
600ml/1 pint/2½ cups stock
225g/8oz can creamed sweetcorn
salt and ground black pepper
finely chopped spring onions,
   to garnish

1 Flake the crab meat roughly with chopsticks or chop the chicken breast. Mix the crab meat or chicken with the chopped root ginger.

2 Beat the egg whites until frothy, add the milk and cornflour paste and beat again until smooth. Blend with the crab meat or chicken breast.

3 Bring the stock to the boil in a wok. Add the creamed sweetcorn and bring back to the boil once more.

4 Stir in the crab meat or chicken breast and egg-white mixture, adjust the seasoning and simmer gently until cooked. Serve garnished with finely chopped spring onions.

Chicken and Asparagus Soup

This is a very delicate and delicious soup, with chicken and asparagus simply and quickly prepared in a wok.

INGREDIENTS

Serves 4
150g/5oz chicken breast fillet
5ml/1 tsp egg white
5ml/1 tsp cornflour paste
115g/4oz fresh or canned asparagus
750ml/1¼ pints/3 cups stock
salt and ground black pepper
fresh coriander leaves, to garnish

1 Cut the chicken meat into thin slices, each about the size of a postage stamp. Mix with a pinch of salt, then add the egg white and finally the cornflour paste.

2 Discard the tough stems of the asparagus, and cut the tender spears diagonally into short lengths.

3 Bring the stock to a rolling boil in a wok. Add the asparagus, bring back to the boil and cook for 2 minutes. (This is not necessary if you are using canned asparagus.)

4 Add the chicken, stir to separate and bring back to the boil once more. Adjust the seasoning to taste. Serve hot, garnished with fresh coriander leaves.

Hot-and-sour Soup

This must surely be the best-known and all-time favourite soup in Chinese restaurants and take-aways throughout the world. It is fairly simple to make once you have got all the necessary ingredients together.

INGREDIENTS

Serves 4

4–6 dried Chinese mushrooms, soaked
   in warm water
115g/4oz pork or chicken
1 packet tofu
50g/2oz sliced bamboo shoots, drained
600ml/1pint/2½ cups stock
15ml/1 tbsp Chinese rice wine or
   dry sherry
15ml/1 tbsp light soy sauce
15ml/1 tbsp rice vinegar
salt and ground white pepper
15ml/1 tbsp cornflour paste

1 Squeeze the soaked mushrooms dry, then discard the hard stalks. Thinly shred the mushrooms, meat, tofu and bamboo shoots.

2 Bring the stock to a rolling boil in a wok and add the shredded ingredients. Bring back to the boil and simmer for about 1 minute.

3 Add the wine or sherry, soy sauce and vinegar and season. Bring back to the boil, then add the cornflour paste, stir until thickened and serve.

Wonton Flowers with Sweet-and-sour Sauce

These melt-in-the-mouth, crisp dumplings make a delicious first course or snack – and take hardly any time at all to prepare.

INGREDIENTS

Serves 4–6
16–20 wonton wrappers
vegetable oil, for deep-frying

For the sauce
15ml/1 tbsp vegetable oil
30ml/2 tbsp light brown sugar
45ml/3 tbsp rice vinegar
15ml/1 tbsp light soy sauce
15ml/1 tbsp tomato ketchup
45–60ml/3–4 tbsp stock or water
15ml/1 tbsp cornflour paste

1 Pinch the centre of each wonton wrapper and twist it around to form a floral shape.

2 Heat the oil in a wok and deep-fry the floral wontons for 1–2 minutes, until crisp. Remove and drain on kitchen paper.

3 To make the sauce, heat the oil in a wok or frying pan and add the sugar, vinegar, soy sauce, tomato ketchup and stock or water.

4 Stir in the cornflour paste to thicken the sauce. Continue stirring until smooth. Pour a little sauce over the wontons and serve immediately with the remaining sauce.

Seafood Wontons with Coriander Dressing

These tasty wontons resemble tortellini. Water chestnuts add a light crunch to the filling.

INGREDIENTS

Serves 4
225g/8oz raw prawns, peeled
  and deveined
115g/4oz white crabmeat, picked over
4 canned water chestnuts, finely diced
1 spring onion, finely chopped
1 small green chilli, seeded and
  finely chopped
2.5ml/½ tsp grated fresh root ginger
1 egg, separated
20–24 wonton wrappers
salt and ground black pepper
coriander leaves, to garnish

For the coriander dressing
30ml/2 tbsp rice vinegar
15ml/1 tbsp chopped pickled ginger
90ml/6 tbsp olive oil
15ml/1 tbsp soy sauce
45ml/3 tbsp chopped coriander
30ml/2 tbsp finely diced red pepper

1 Finely dice the prawns and place them in a bowl. Add the crabmeat, water chestnuts, spring onion, chilli, ginger and egg white. Season with salt and pepper and stir well.

2 Place a wonton wrapper on a board. Put about 5ml/1 tsp of the filling just above the centre of the wrapper. With a pastry brush, moisten the edges of the wrapper with a little of the egg yolk. Bring the bottom of the wrapper up over the filling. Press gently to expel any air, then seal the wrapper neatly in a triangle.

3 For a more elaborate shape, bring the two side points up over the filling, overlap the points and pinch the ends firmly together. Space the filled wontons on a large baking sheet lined with greaseproof paper, so that they do not stick together.

4 Half fill a large saucepan with water. Bring to simmering point. Add the filled wontons, a few at a time, and simmer for 2–3 minutes. The wontons will float to the surface. When ready the wrappers will be translucent and the filling should be cooked. Remove the wontons with a large slotted spoon, drain them briefly, then spread them on trays. Keep warm while cooking the remaining wontons.

5 Make the coriander dressing by whisking all the ingredients together in a bowl. Divide the wontons among serving dishes, drizzle with the dressing and serve garnished with a handful of coriander leaves.

Steamed Seafood Packets

Very neat and delicate, these steamed packets make an excellent starter or a light lunch.

INGREDIENTS
Serves 4
225g/8oz crab meat
50g/2oz shelled prawns, chopped
6 water chestnuts, chopped
30ml/2 tbsp chopped bamboo shoots
15ml/1 tbsp chopped spring onion
5ml/1 tsp chopped root ginger
15ml/1 tbsp soy sauce
15ml/1 tbsp fish sauce
12 rice sheets
banana leaves
oil for brushing
15ml/1 tbsp soy sauce
2 spring onions, shredded, to garnish
2 red chillies, seeded and sliced, to garnish
coriander leaves, to garnish

1 Combine the crab meat, chopped prawns, chestnuts, bamboo shoots, spring onion and ginger in a bowl. Mix well, then add the soy sauce and fish sauce. Stir until blended.

2 Take a rice sheet and dip it in warm water. Place it on a flat surface and leave for a few seconds to soften.

COOK'S TIP

The seafood packets will spread out when steamed so be sure to space them well apart to prevent them sticking together.

3 Place a spoonful of the filling in the centre of the sheet and fold into a square packet. Repeat with the rest of the rice sheets and seafood mixture.

4 Use banana leaves to line a steamer, then brush them with oil. Place the packets, seam-side down, on the leaves and steam over a high heat for 6–8 minutes or until the filling is cooked. Transfer to a plate and garnish with the remaining ingredients.

Mini Spring Rolls

Eat these irresistibly light and crisp parcels with your fingers. If you like slightly spicier food, sprinkle them with a little cayenne pepper before serving.

INGREDIENTS

Makes 20
1 green chilli
120ml/4fl oz/½ cup vegetable oil
1 small onion, finely chopped
1 garlic clove, crushed
75g/3oz cooked boneless chicken
    breast, skinned
1 small carrot, cut into fine matchsticks
1 spring onion, finely sliced
1 small red pepper, seeded and cut into
    fine matchsticks
25g/1oz beansprouts
5ml/1 tsp sesame oil
4 large sheets filo pastry
1 small egg white, lightly beaten
long chives, to garnish (optional)
45ml/3 tbsp light soy sauce, to serve

1 Carefully remove the seeds from the chilli and chop finely, wearing rubber gloves to protect your hands, if necessary.

2 Heat 30ml/2 tbsp of the vegetable oil in a preheated wok. Add the onion, garlic and chilli and stir-fry for 1 minute.

3 Slice the chicken breast very thinly, then add to the wok and fry over a high heat, stirring constantly, until browned.

4 Add the carrot, spring onion and red pepper and stir-fry for 2 minutes. Add the beansprouts, stir in the sesame oil and leave to cool.

5 Cut each sheet of filo pastry into 5 short strips. Place a small amount of filling at one end of each strip, then fold in the long sides and roll up the pastry. Seal and glaze the parcels with the egg white, then chill, uncovered, for 15 minutes before frying.

6 Wipe the wok with kitchen paper, reheat it and add the remaining vegetable oil. When the oil is hot, fry the rolls in batches until crisp and golden brown. Drain on kitchen paper and serve dipped in light soy sauce.

COOK'S TIP

Be careful to avoid touching your face or eyes when seeding and chopping chillies because they are very potent and may cause burning and irritation to the skin. Try preparing chillies under running water.

Root Vegetables with Spiced Salt

All kinds of root vegetables can be finely sliced and deep fried to make "crisps". Serve as an accompaniment to an oriental-style meal or simply by themselves as much tastier nibbles than commercial snacks with pre-dinner drinks.

INGREDIENTS

Serves 4–6
1 carrot
2 parsnips
2 raw beetroots
1 sweet potato
groundnut oil, for deep frying
1.5ml/¼ tsp chilli powder
5ml/1 tsp sea salt flakes

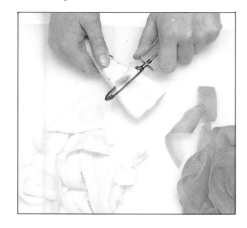

1 Peel the carrot, parsnips, beetroots and sweet potato. Slice the carrot and parsnips into long, thin ribbons. Cut the beetroots and sweet potato into thin rounds. Pat dry on kitchen paper.

2 Half-fill a wok with oil and heat to 180°C/350°F. Add the vegetable slices in batches and deep-fry for 2–3 minutes until golden and crisp. Remove and drain on kitchen paper.

3 Place the chilli powder and sea salt flakes in a mortar and grind them together with a pestle to form a coarse powder.

4 Pile up the vegetable "crisps" on a serving plate and sprinkle over the spiced salt.

— COOK'S TIP —

To save time, you can slice the vegetables using a mandoline, blender or food processor with a thin slicing disc attached.

Crispy "Seaweed"

Surprisingly, the very popular and rather exotic-sounding "seaweed" served in Chinese restaurants is, in fact, just ordinary spring greens.

INGREDIENTS

Serves 4
450g/1lb spring greens
vegetable oil, for deep frying
2.5ml/¹/₂ tsp salt
5ml/1 tsp caster sugar
15ml/1 tbsp ground fried fish, to
garnish (optional)

1 Cut off the hard stalks in the centre of each spring green leaf. Pile the leaves on top of each other, and roll into a tight sausage shape. Thinly cut the leaves into fine shreds. Spread them out to dry.

2 Heat the oil in a wok until hot. Deep fry the shredded greens in batches, stirring to separate them.

3 Remove the greens with a slotted spoon as soon as they are crispy, but before they turn brown. Drain. Sprinkle the salt and sugar evenly all over the "seaweed", mix well, garnish with ground fish, if liked, and serve.

Sesame Seed Prawn Toasts

Use uncooked prawns for this dish, as ready-cooked ones will tend to separate from the bread during cooking.

INGREDIENTS

Serves 4
225g/8oz uncooked prawns, peeled
25g/1oz lard
1 egg white, lightly beaten
5ml/1 tsp finely chopped spring onions
2.5ml/¹/₂ tsp finely chopped
root ginger
15ml/1 tbsp Chinese rice wine or
dry sherry
15ml/1 tbsp cornflour paste
115–150g/4–5oz/white
sesame seeds
6 large slices white bread
vegetable oil, for deep frying
salt and ground black pepper

1 Chop together the prawns with the lard to form a smooth paste. In a bowl, mix with all the other ingredients except the sesame seeds and bread.

2 Spread the sesame seeds evenly on a large plate or tray; spread the prawn paste thickly on one side of each slice of bread, then press, spread side down, on to the seeds.

3 Heat the oil in a wok until medium-hot; fry 2–3 slices of the sesame bread at a time, spread side down, for 2–3 minutes. Remove and drain. Cut each slice into six or eight fingers (without crusts).

FISH &
SEAFOOD

Chinese-spiced Fish Fillets

INGREDIENTS

Serves 4

65g/2½oz/generous ½ cup plain flour
5ml/1 tsp Chinese five-spice powder
8 skinless fillets of fish, such as plaice or
  lemon sole, about 800g/1¾lb in total
1 egg, lightly beaten
40–50g/1½–2oz/scant 1 cup fine
  fresh breadcrumbs
groundnut oil, for frying
25g/1oz/2 tbsp butter
4 spring onions, cut diagonally into
  thin slices
350g/12oz tomatoes, seeded and diced
30ml/2 tbsp soy sauce
salt and ground black pepper
red pepper strips and chives, to garnish

1 Sift the flour together with the
Chinese five-spice powder and salt
and pepper to taste on to a plate. Dip
the fish fillets first in the seasoned flour,
then in the beaten egg and finally in
breadcrumbs.

2 Pour oil into a large frying pan to a
depth of 1cm/½ in. Heat until it is
very hot and starting to sizzle. Add the
coated fillets, a few at a time, and fry
for 2–3 minutes on each side,
depending on their thickness, until just
cooked and golden brown. Do not
crowd the pan, or the temperature of
the oil will drop and the fish will
absorb too much of it.

3 Drain the fillets on kitchen paper,
then transfer to serving plates and
keep warm. Pour off all the oil from
the frying pan and wipe it out with
kitchen paper.

4 Cook the spring onions and
tomatoes in the butter for 1 minute,
then add the soy sauce.

5 Spoon the tomato mixture over
the fish, garnish with red pepper
strips and chives and serve.

Steamed Fish with Ginger and Spring Onions

Firm and delicate fish steaks, such as salmon or turbot, can be cooked by this same method.

INGREDIENTS

Serves 4–6

1 sea bass, trout or grey mullet, weighing about 675g/1½lb, gutted
2.5ml/½ tsp salt
15ml/1 tbsp sesame oil
2–3 spring onions, cut in half lengthways
30ml/2 tbsp light soy sauce
30ml/2 tbsp Chinese rice wine or dry sherry
15ml/1 tbsp finely shredded fresh ginger
30ml/2 tbsp vegetable oil
finely shredded spring onions, to garnish

1 Using a sharp knife, score both sides of the fish as far down as the bone with diagonal cuts about 2.5cm/1in apart. Rub the fish all over, inside and out, with salt and sesame oil.

2 Sprinkle the spring onions over a heatproof platter and place the fish on top. Blend together the soy sauce and rice wine or dry sherry with the ginger shreds and pour evenly all over the fish.

3 Place the platter in a very hot steamer (or inside a wok on a rack) and steam vigorously, under cover, for 12–15 minutes.

4 Heat the vegetable oil until hot. Remove the platter from the steamer, place the shredded spring onions on top of the fish, then pour the hot oil along the whole length of the fish. Serve immediately.

Sweet-and-sour Fish

When fish is cooked in this way the skin becomes crispy on the outside, while the flesh remains moist and juicy inside. The sweet and sour sauce, with its colourful cherry tomatoes, complements the fish beautifully.

INGREDIENTS

Serves 4–6

1 large or 2 medium-size fish such as snapper or mullet, heads removed
20ml/4 tsp cornflour
120ml/4fl oz/½ cup vegetable oil
15ml/1 tbsp chopped garlic
15ml/1 tbsp chopped root ginger
30ml/2 tbsp chopped shallots
225g/8oz cherry tomatoes
30ml/2 tbsp red wine vinegar
30ml/2 tbsp granulated sugar
30ml/2 tbsp tomato ketchup
15ml/1 tbsp fish sauce
45ml/3 tbsp water
salt and freshly ground black pepper
coriander leaves, to garnish
shredded spring onions, to garnish

1 Thoroughly rinse and clean the fish. Score the skin diagonally on both sides of the fish.

2 Coat the fish lightly on both sides with 15ml/1 tbsp cornflour. Shake off any excess.

3 Heat the oil in a wok or large frying pan and slide the fish into the wok. Reduce the heat to medium and fry the fish until crisp and brown, about 6–7 minutes on both sides.

4 Remove the fish with a fish slice and place on a large platter.

5 Pour off all but 30ml/2 tbsp of the oil and add the garlic, ginger and shallots. Fry until golden.

6 Add the cherry tomatoes and cook until they burst open. Stir in the vinegar, sugar, tomato ketchup and fish sauce. Simmer gently for 1–2 minutes and adjust the seasoning.

7 Blend the remaining 5ml/1 tsp cornflour with the water. Stir into the sauce and heat until it thickens. Pour the sauce over the fish and garnish with coriander leaves and shredded spring onions.

Braised Fish Fillet with Mushrooms

This is the Chinese stir-fried version of the French *filets de sole bonne femme* (sole cooked with mushrooms and wine sauce).

INGREDIENTS

Serves 4
450g/1lb lemon sole or plaice fillets
5ml/1 tsp salt
1/2 egg white
30ml/2 tbsp cornflour paste
about 600ml/1 pint/2½ cups
   vegetable oil
15ml/1 tbsp finely chopped
   spring onions
2.5ml/½ tsp finely chopped fresh
   root ginger
115g/4oz white mushrooms,
   thinly sliced
5ml/1 tsp light brown sugar
15ml/1 tbsp light soy sauce
30ml/2 tbsp Chinese rice wine or
   dry sherry
15ml/1 tbsp brandy
about 120ml/4fl oz/⅔ cup stock
few drops sesame oil

1 Trim off the soft bones along the edge of the fish, but leave the skin on. Cut each fillet into bite-sized pieces. Mix the fish with a little salt, the egg white and about half of the cornflour paste.

COOK'S TIP

You could substitute straw mushrooms, so called because they are grown on beds of rice straw. They have a subtle flavour and a slightly slippery texture.

2 Heat the oil in a preheated wok until medium-hot, add the fish, slice by slice, and stir gently so the pieces do not stick. Remove after about 1 minute and drain. Pour off the excess oil, leaving about 30ml/2 tbsp in the wok.

3 Stir-fry the spring onions, ginger and mushrooms for 1 minute. Add the sugar, soy sauce, rice wine or sherry, brandy and stock. Bring to the boil. Return the fish to the wok and braise for 1 minute. Stir in the remaining cornflour paste to thicken the sauce and sprinkle with sesame oil.

Prawn Fu-yung

This is a very colourful dish that is simple to make in a wok. Most of the preparation can be done well in advance.

INGREDIENTS

Serves 4
3 eggs, beaten, reserving 5ml/1 tsp
   egg white
15ml/1 tbsp finely chopped
   spring onions
45–60ml/3–4 tbsp vegetable oil
225g/8oz uncooked prawns, peeled
10ml/2 tsp cornflour paste
175g/6oz green peas
15ml/1 tbsp Chinese rice wine or
   dry sherry
salt

1 Beat the eggs with a pinch of the salt and a few pieces of the spring onions. Heat a little oil in a preheated wok over a moderate heat. Add the egg mixture and stir to scramble. Remove the scrambled eggs and reserve.

2 Mix the prawns with a little salt, 5ml/1 tsp egg white and the cornflour paste. Stir-fry the peas in hot oil for 30 seconds Add the prawns.

3 Add the spring onions. Stir-fry for 1 minute, then stir the mixture into the scrambled egg with a little salt and the wine or sherry and serve.

Stir-fried Prawns with Broccoli

This is a very colourful dish, highly nutritious and at the same time extremely delicious; furthermore, it is not time-consuming or difficult to prepare.

INGREDIENTS

Serves 4

175–225g/6–8oz prawns, shelled
  and deveined
5ml/1 tsp salt
15ml/1 tbsp Chinese rice wine or
  dry sherry
¹/₂ egg white
15ml/1 tbsp cornflour paste
225g/8oz broccoli
about 300ml/¹/₂ pint/1¹/₄ cups
  vegetable oil
1 spring onion, cut into
  short sections
5ml/1 tsp light brown sugar
about 30ml/2 tbsp stock or water
5ml/1 tsp light soy sauce
few drops sesame oil

1 Cut each prawn in half lengthways. Mix with a pinch of salt and about 5ml/1 tsp of the rice wine, egg white and cornflour paste.

2 Cut the broccoli heads into florets; remove the rough skin from the stalks, then slice the florets diagonally into diamond-shaped chunks.

3 Heat the oil in a preheated wok and stir-fry the prawns for about 30 seconds. Remove with a slotted spoon and drain thoroughly.

4 Pour off the excess oil, leaving 30ml/2 tbsp in the wok. Add the broccoli and spring onion, stir-fry for about 2 minutes, then add the remaining salt and the sugar, followed by the prawns and stock or water. Add the soy sauce and remaining rice wine or sherry. Blend well, then finally add the sesame oil and serve.

Gingered Seafood Stir-fry

This cornucopia of scallops, prawns and squid in an aromatic sauce makes a refreshing summer supper, served with plenty of crusty bread to mop up the juices – together with a glass of chilled dry white wine. It would also make a great dinner-party starter for four people.

INGREDIENTS

Serves 2

15ml/1 tbsp sunflower oil
5ml/1 tsp sesame oil
2.5cm/1in fresh root ginger,
　finely chopped
1 bunch spring onions, sliced
1 red pepper, seeded and finely
　chopped
115g/4 oz small queen scallops
8 large raw prawns, peeled
115g/4oz squid rings
15ml/1 tbsp lime juice
15ml/1 tbsp light soy sauce
60ml/4 tbsp coconut milk
salt and ground black pepper
mixed salad leaves and lime slices,
　to serve

1 Heat the sunflower and sesame oils in a preheated wok or large frying pan and cook the ginger and spring onions for 2–3 minutes, or until golden. Stir in the red pepper and cook for a further 3 minutes.

2 Add the scallops, prawns and squid rings and cook over a medium heat for about 3 minutes, until the seafood is just cooked.

3 Stir in the lime juice, soy sauce and coconut milk. Simmer, uncovered, for 2 minutes, until the juices begin to thicken slightly.

4 Season well. Arrange the salad leaves on 2 serving plates and spoon over the seafood mixture with the juices. Serve with lime slices for squeezing over the seafood.

Red and White Prawns with Green Vegetables

The Chinese name for this dish is *Yuan Yang* prawns. Pairs of mandarin ducks are also known as *yuan yang*, or love birds, because they are always seen together. They symbolize affection and happiness.

INGREDIENTS

Serves 4–6
450g/1lb raw prawns
½ egg white
15ml/1 tbsp cornflour paste
175g/6oz mangetouts
about 600ml/1 pint/2½ cups
 vegetable oil
5ml/1 tsp light brown sugar
15ml/1 tbsp finely chopped spring
 onion
5ml/1 tsp finely chopped fresh root
 ginger
15ml/1 tbsp light soy sauce
15ml/1 tbsp Chinese rice wine or
 dry sherry
5ml/1 tsp chilli bean sauce
15ml/1 tbsp tomato purée
salt

1 Peel and devein the prawns and mix with the egg white, cornflour paste and a pinch of salt. Top and tail the mangetouts.

2 Heat 30–45ml/2–3 tbsp of the oil in a preheated wok and stir-fry the mangetouts for about 1 minute. Add the sugar and a little salt and continue stirring for 1 more minute. Remove and place in the centre of a warmed serving platter.

3 Add the remaining oil to the wok and cook the prawns for 1 minute. Remove and drain.

4 Pour off all but about 15ml/1 tbsp of the oil. Add the spring onion and ginger to the wok.

5 Return the prawns to the wok and stir-fry for 1 minute, then add the soy sauce and rice wine or dry sherry. Blend the mixture thoroughly. Transfer half the prawns to one end of the serving platter.

6 Add the chilli bean sauce and tomato purée to the remaining prawns in the wok, blend well and place the "red" prawns at the other end of the platter. Serve.

COOK'S TIP

All raw prawns have an intestinal tract that runs just beneath the outside curve of the tail. The tract is not poisonous, but it can taste unpleasant. It is, therefore, best to remove it – devein. To do this, peel the prawns, leaving the tail intact. Score each prawn lightly along its length to expose the tract. Remove the tract with a small knife or Chinese cleaver.

Chilli Prawns

This delightful, spicy combination makes a lovely, light main course for a casual supper. Serve with rice, noodles or even freshly cooked pasta and a leafy green salad.

INGREDIENTS

Serves 3–4
45ml/3 tbsp olive oil
2 shallots, chopped
2 garlic cloves, chopped
1 fresh red chilli, chopped
450g/1lb ripe tomatoes, skinned, seeded and chopped
15ml/1 tbsp tomato purée
1 bay leaf
1 thyme sprig
90ml/6 tbsp dry white wine
450g/1lb cooked large prawns, peeled
salt and ground black pepper
roughly torn basil leaves, to garnish

1 Heat the oil in a pan, then add the shallots, garlic and chilli and fry until the garlic starts to brown.

2 Add the tomatoes, tomato purée, bay leaf, thyme, wine and seasoning. Bring to the boil, then reduce the heat and cook gently for about 10 minutes, stirring occasionally, until the sauce has thickened. Discard the herbs.

3 Stir the prawns into the sauce and heat through for a few minutes. Taste and adjust the seasoning. Scatter over the basil leaves and serve at once.

COOK'S TIP

For a milder flavour, remove all the seeds from the chilli.

Scallops with Ginger

Scallops are at their best in the winter, but are available frozen throughout the year. Rich and creamy, this dish is very simple to make and utterly scrumptious.

INGREDIENTS

Serves 4
8–12 scallops, shelled
40g/1½oz/3 tbsp butter
2.5cm/1in fresh root ginger, finely chopped
1 bunch spring onions, sliced diagonally
60ml/4 tbsp white vermouth
250ml/8fl oz/1 cup crème fraîche
salt and ground black pepper
chopped fresh parsley, to garnish

1 Remove the tough muscle opposite the coral on each scallop. Separate the coral and cut the white part of the scallop in half horizontally.

2 Melt the butter in a frying pan. Add the scallops, including the corals, and sauté for about 2 minutes until lightly browned. Take care not to overcook the scallops as this will make them tough.

3 Lift out the scallops with a slotted spoon and transfer to a warmed serving dish. Keep warm.

4 Add the ginger and spring onions to the pan and stir-fry for 2 minutes. Pour in the vermouth and allow to bubble until it has almost evaporated. Stir in the crème fraîche and cook for a few minutes until the sauce has thickened. Taste and adjust the seasoning.

5 Pour the sauce over the scallops, sprinkle with parsley and serve immediately.

Baked Lobster with Black Beans

The term "baked", as used on most Chinese restaurant menus, is not strictly correct – "pot-roasted" or "pan-baked" is more accurate.

INGREDIENTS

Serves 4–6

1 large or 2 medium lobsters, about 800g/1¾lb in total
vegetable oil, for deep-frying
1 garlic clove, finely chopped
5ml/1 tsp finely chopped fresh root ginger
2–3 spring onions, chopped
30ml/2 tbsp black bean sauce
30ml/2 tbsp Chinese rice wine or dry sherry
120ml/4fl oz/½ cup stock or water
fresh coriander leaves, to garnish

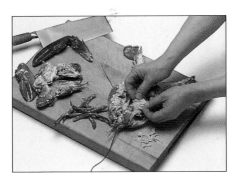

1 Starting from the head, cut the lobster in half lengthways. Discard the legs, remove the claws and crack them with the back of a cleaver. Discard the feathery lungs and intestine. Cut each half into 4–5 pieces.

2 Heat the oil in a preheated wok and deep-fry the lobster pieces for about 2 minutes, or until the shells turn bright orange. Remove the pieces from the wok and drain on kitchen paper.

3 Pour off the excess oil, leaving about 15ml/1 tbsp in the wok. Add the garlic, ginger, spring onions and black bean sauce and stir-fry for 1 minute.

4 Add the lobster pieces to the sauce and blend well. Add the rice wine or dry sherry and stock, bring to the boil, cover and cook for 2–3 minutes. Serve garnished with coriander leaves.

COOK'S TIP

Ideally, buy live lobsters and cook them yourself. Ready-cooked ones have usually been boiled for far too long and have lost much of their delicate flavour and texture.

Stir-fried Five-spice Squid

Squid is perfect for stir-frying as it should be cooked quickly. The spicy sauce makes the ideal accompaniment.

INGREDIENTS

Serves 6

450g/1lb small squid, cleaned
45ml/3 tbsp oil
2.5cm/1 in fresh root ginger, grated
1 garlic clove, crushed
8 spring onions, cut diagonally into
   2.5cm/1in lengths
1 red pepper, seeded and cut into strips
1 fresh green chilli, seeded and thinly
   sliced
6 mushrooms, sliced
5ml/1 tsp Chinese five-spice powder
30ml/2 tbsp black bean sauce
30ml/2 tbsp soy sauce
5ml/1 tsp sugar
15ml/1 tbsp Chinese rice wine or
   dry sherry

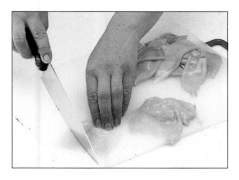

1 Rinse the squid and pull away the outer skin. Dry on kitchen paper. Slit the squid open and score the inside into diamonds with a sharp knife. Cut the squid into strips.

2 Heat the oil in a preheated wok. Stir-fry the squid quickly. Remove the squid strips from the wok with a slotted spoon and set aside. Add the ginger, garlic, spring onions, red pepper, chilli and mushrooms to the oil remaining in the wok and stir-fry for 2 minutes.

3 Return the squid to the wok and stir in the five-spice powder. Stir in the black bean sauce, soy sauce, sugar and rice wine or dry sherry. Bring to the boil and cook, stirring, for 1 minute. Serve immediately.

Clay Pot of Chilli Squid and Noodles

INGREDIENTS

Serves 4

675g/1½lb fresh squid
30ml/2 tbsp vegetable oil
3 slices fresh root ginger,
   finely shredded
2 garlic cloves, finely chopped
1 red onion, finely sliced
1 carrot, finely sliced
1 celery stick, diagonally sliced
50g/2oz sugar snap peas, topped
   and tailed
5ml/1 tsp sugar
15ml/1 tbsp chilli bean paste
2.5ml/½ tsp chilli powder
75g/3oz cellophane noodles, soaked in
   hot water until soft
120ml/4fl oz/½ cup chicken stock
   or water
15ml/1 tbsp soy sauce
15ml/1 tbsp oyster sauce
5ml/1 tsp sesame oil
pinch of salt
coriander leaves, to garnish

1 Prepare the squid. Holding the body in one hand, gently pull away the head and tentacles. Discard the head; trim and reserve the tentacles. Remove the transparent "quill" from inside the body of the squid. Peel off the brown skin on the outside of the body. Rub a little salt into the squid and wash thoroughly under cold running water. Cut the body of the squid into rings or split it open lengthways, score criss-cross patterns on the inside of the body and cut it into 5 x 4cm/2 x 1½in pieces.

2 Heat the oil in a large clay pot or flameproof casserole. Add the ginger, garlic and onion, and fry for 1–2 minutes. Add the squid, carrot, celery and sugar snap peas. Fry until the squid curls up. Season with salt and sugar, and stir in the chilli bean paste and powder. Transfer the mixture to a bowl and set aside until required.

3 Drain the soaked noodles and add them to the clay pot or casserole. Stir in the stock or water, soy sauce and oyster sauce. Cover and cook over a medium heat for about 10 minutes or until the noodles are tender.

4 Return the squid and vegetables to the pot. Cover and cook for about 5–6 minutes more, until all the flavours are combined. Season to taste.

5 Just before serving, drizzle with the sesame oil and sprinkle with the coriander leaves.

— Cook's Tip —

These noodles have a smooth, light texture that readily absorbs the other flavours in the dish. To vary the flavour, the vegetables can be altered according to what is available.

Squid with Green Pepper and Black Bean Sauce

This dish is a product of the Cantonese school and makes an attractive meal that is just as delicious as it looks.

INGREDIENTS

Serves 4

375–400g/12–14oz squid
1 medium green pepper, cored and seeded
45–60ml/3–4 tbsp vegetable oil
1 garlic clove, finely chopped
2.5ml/½ tsp finely chopped fresh root ginger
15ml/1 tbsp finely chopped spring onion
5ml/1 tsp salt
15ml/1 tbsp black bean sauce
15ml/1 tbsp Chinese rice wine or dry sherry
few drops of sesame oil

1 To clean the squid, cut off the tentacles just below the eye. Remove the "quill" from inside the body. Peel off and discard the skin, then wash the squid and dry well. Cut open the squid and score the inside of the flesh in a criss-cross pattern.

2 Cut the squid into pieces each about the size of an oblong postage stamp. Blanch the squid in a pan of boiling water for a few seconds. Remove and drain. Dry well.

3 Cut the green pepper into small triangular pieces. Heat the oil in a preheated wok and stir-fry the green pepper for about 1 minute.

4 Add the garlic, ginger, spring onion, salt and squid, then stir for 1 minute. Add the black bean sauce, rice wine or dry sherry and sesame oil and serve.

MEAT &
POULTRY

Pork Chow Mein

A perfect, speedy meal, this family favourite is flavoured with sesame oil for an authentic oriental taste.

INGREDIENTS

Serves 4

175g/6oz medium egg noodles
350g/12oz pork fillet
30ml/2 tbsp sunflower oil
15ml/1 tbsp sesame oil
2 garlic cloves, crushed
8 spring onions, sliced
1 red pepper, seeded and roughly chopped
1 green pepper, seeded and roughly chopped
30ml/2 tbsp dark soy sauce
45ml/3 tbsp Chinese rice wine or dry sherry
175g/6oz beansprouts
45ml/3 tbsp chopped fresh flat-leaf parsley
15ml/1 tbsp toasted sesame seeds

1 Soak the noodles according to the packet instructions. Drain well.

2 Thinly slice the pork fillet. Heat the sunflower oil in a preheated wok or large frying pan and cook the pork over a high heat until golden brown and cooked through.

3 Add the sesame oil to the wok or frying pan, with the garlic, spring onions and peppers. Cook over a high heat for 3–4 minutes, or until the vegetables are beginning to soften.

4 Reduce the heat slightly and stir in the noodles, with the soy sauce and rice wine or dry sherry. Stir-fry for 2 minutes. Add the beansprouts and cook for a further 1–2 minutes. If the noodles begin to stick, add a splash of water. Stir in the parsley and serve sprinkled with the sesame seeds.

Lemon Grass Pork

Chillies and lemon grass flavour this simple stir-fry, while peanuts add crunch.

INGREDIENTS

Serves 4

675g/1½lb boneless loin of pork
2 lemon grass stalks, finely chopped
4 spring onions, thinly sliced
5ml/1 tsp salt
12 black peppercorns, coarsely crushed
30ml/2 tbsp groundnut oil
2 garlic cloves, chopped
2 fresh red chillies, seeded and chopped
5ml/1 tsp light brown soft sugar
30ml/2 tbsp Thai fish sauce (*nam pla*),
   or to taste
25g/1oz roasted unsalted
   peanuts, chopped
salt and ground black pepper
coriander leaves, to garnish
rice noodles, to serve

1 Trim any excess fat from the pork. Cut the meat across into 5mm/¼in thick slices, then cut each slice into 5mm/¼in strips. Put the pork into a bowl with the lemon grass, spring onions, salt and crushed peppercorns. Mix well, then cover and leave to marinate for 30 minutes.

2 Heat a wok until hot, add the oil and swirl it around. Add the pork mixture and stir-fry for 3 minutes.

3 Add the garlic and chillies and stir-fry for a further 5–8 minutes over a medium heat until the pork no longer looks pink.

4 Add the sugar, fish sauce and chopped peanuts and toss to mix. Taste and adjust the seasoning, if necessary. Serve at once, garnished with roughly torn coriander leaves on a bed of rice noodles.

Pork and Vegetable Stir-fry

A quick and easy stir-fry of pork and a mixture of vegetables, this makes an excellent family lunch or supper dish.

INGREDIENTS

Serves 4

225g/8oz can pineapple chunks
15ml/1 tbsp cornflour
30ml/2 tbsp light soy sauce
15ml/1 tbsp Chinese rice wine or
  dry sherry
15ml/1 tbsp soft brown sugar
15ml/1 tbsp white wine vinegar
5ml/1 tsp Chinese five-spice powder
10ml/2 tsp olive oil
1 red onion, sliced
1 garlic clove, crushed
1 fresh red chilli, seeded and chopped
2.5cm/1in fresh root ginger
350g/12oz lean pork tenderloin, cut
  into thin strips
175g/6oz carrots
1 red pepper, seeded and sliced
175g/6oz mangetouts, halved
115g/4oz beansprouts
200g/7oz can sweetcorn kernels
30ml/2 tbsp chopped fresh coriander
salt
15ml/1 tbsp toasted sesame seeds,
  to garnish

1 Drain the pineapple, reserving the juice. In a small bowl, blend the cornflour with the reserved pineapple juice. Add the soy sauce, rice wine or dry sherry, sugar, vinegar and five-spice powder, stir to mix and set aside.

2 Heat the oil in a preheated wok or large, non-stick frying pan. Add the onion, garlic, chilli and ginger and stir-fry for 30 seconds. Add the pork and stir-fry for 2–3 minutes.

3 Cut the carrots into matchstick strips. Add to the wok with the red pepper and stir-fry for 2–3 minutes. Add the mangetouts, beansprouts and sweetcorn and stir-fry for 1–2 minutes.

4 Pour in the sauce mixture and the reserved pineapple and stir-fry until the sauce thickens. Reduce the heat and stir-fry for a further 1–2 minutes. Stir in the coriander and season to taste. Sprinkle with sesame seeds and serve immediately.

Stuffed Green Peppers

Stuffed peppers are given a different treatment here where they are deep fried in a wok and served with a tangy sauce.

INGREDIENTS

Serves 4

225–275g/8–10oz minced pork
4–6 water chestnuts, finely chopped
2 spring onions, finely chopped
2.5ml/½ tsp finely chopped fresh
   root ginger
15ml/1 tbsp light soy sauce
15ml/1 tbsp Chinese rice wine or
   dry sherry
3–4 green peppers, cored and seeded
15ml/1 tbsp cornflour
vegetable oil, for deep frying

For the sauce

10ml/2 tsp light soy sauce
5ml/1 tsp light brown sugar
1–2 fresh hot chillies, finely
   chopped (optional)
about 75ml/5 tbsp stock or water

1 Mix together the minced pork, water chestnuts, spring onions, ginger, soy sauce and rice wine or sherry in a bowl.

COOK'S TIP

You could substitute minced beef or lamb for the minced pork used in this recipe.

2 Cut the green peppers into halves or quarters. Stuff the sections with the pork mixture and sprinkle with a little cornflour.

3 Heat the oil in a preheated wok and deep fry the stuffed peppers, with the meat side down, for 2–3 minutes, then remove and drain.

4 Pour off the excess oil, then return the stuffed green peppers to the wok with the meat side up. Add the sauce ingredients, shaking the wok gently to make sure they do not stick to the bottom, and braise for 2–3 minutes. Carefully lift the stuffed peppers on to a serving dish, meat side up, and pour the sauce over them.

Stir-fried Beef and Broccoli

This spicy beef may be served with noodles or on a bed of boiled rice for a speedy and low-calorie Chinese meal.

INGREDIENTS

Serves 4

350g/12oz rump steak
15ml/1 tbsp cornflour
5ml/1 tsp sesame oil
350g/12oz broccoli, cut into small florets
4 spring onions, sliced diagonally
1 carrot, cut into matchstick strips
1 garlic clove, crushed
2.5cm/1in fresh root ginger, cut into very fine strips
120ml/4fl oz/½ cup beef stock
30ml/2 tbsp soy sauce
30ml/2 tbsp dry sherry
10ml/2 tsp soft light brown sugar
spring onion tassels, to garnish (optional)
noodles or rice, to serve

1 Trim the beef and cut into thin slices across the grain. Cut each slice into thin strips. Toss in the cornflour to coat thoroughly.

2 Heat the sesame oil in a preheated wok or large non-stick frying pan. Add the beef strips and stir-fry over a brisk heat for 3 minutes. Remove and set aside.

3 Add the broccoli, spring onions, carrot, garlic, ginger and stock to the wok or frying pan. Cover and simmer for 3 minutes. Uncover and cook, stirring, until all the stock has reduced entirely.

4 Mix the soy sauce, dry sherry and brown sugar together and add to the wok or frying pan with the beef. Cook for 2–3 minutes, stirring continuously. Spoon into a warmed serving dish and garnish with spring onion tassels, if liked. Serve on a bed of noodles or rice.

COOK'S TIP

To make spring onion tassels, trim the bulb base, then cut the green shoot so that the onion is 7.5cm/3in long. Shred to within 2.5cm/1in of the base and put into iced water for 1 hour.

Sizzling Beef with Celeriac Straw

The crisp celeriac matchsticks look like fine pieces of straw when stir-fried, and they have a mild celery-like flavour that is quite delicious.

INGREDIENTS

Serves 4
450g/1lb celeriac
150ml/¼ pint/⅔ cup vegetable oil
1 red pepper
6 spring onions
450g/1lb rump steak
60ml/4 tbsp beef stock
30ml/2 tbsp sherry vinegar
10ml/2 tsp Worcestershire sauce
10ml/2 tsp tomato purée
salt and ground black pepper

1 Peel the celeriac and then cut into fine matchsticks, using a cleaver.

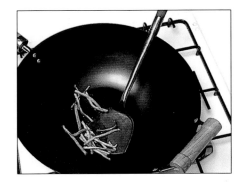

2 Heat a wok, then add two-thirds of the oil. When the oil is hot, fry the celeriac matchsticks in batches until golden brown and crispy. Drain well on kitchen paper.

3 Halve, core and seed the red pepper, then slice diagonally into 2.5cm/1in lengths. Slice the spring onions diagonally into 2.5cm/1in lengths.

4 Chop the beef into thin strips, across the grain of meat.

5 Heat the wok again and add the remaining oil. When the oil is hot, stir-fry the chopped red pepper and spring onion for 2–3 minutes.

6 Add the beef strips and stir-fry for a further 3–4 minutes until browned. Add the stock, vinegar, Worcestershire sauce and tomato purée. Season to taste and serve with the celeriac straw.

COOK'S TIP

Avoid buying very large celeriac roots, as they tend to be woody or otherwise unpleasant in texture. As it is rather an unwieldy and knobbly vegetable, celeriac is easier to peel properly if you cut it into more or less even-sized slices first. Then peel each slice individually using a very sharp knife. They need to be peeled quite thickly to obtain a neat edge. You can then easily cut the slices into thin strips.

Szechuan Spicy Tofu

The meat used in this popular wok recipe can be omitted to create a purely vegetarian dish, if you prefer.

INGREDIENTS

Serves 4

3 packets tofu
1 leek
45ml/3 tbsp vegetable oil
115g/4oz minced beef
15ml/1 tbsp black bean sauce
15ml/1 tbsp light soy sauce
5ml/1 tsp chilli bean sauce
15ml/1 tbsp Chinese rice wine or
  dry sherry
about 45–60ml/3–4 tbsp stock or water
10ml/2 tsp cornflour paste
ground Szechuan peppercorns, to taste
few drops of sesame oil

1 Cut the tofu into 1cm/½in square cubes. Fill a wok with boiling water, add the tofu cubes and bring back to the boil. Cook for 2–3 minutes to harden. Remove and drain. Cut the leek into short sections.

2 Empty the wok. Preheat and add the oil. When hot, stir-fry the minced beef until the colour changes, then add the leek and black bean sauce. Add the tofu with the soy sauce, chilli bean sauce and rice wine or sherry. Stir gently for 1 minute.

3 Add the stock or water, bring to the boil and braise for 2-3 minutes.

4 Stir in the cornflour paste and cook, stirring, until thickened. Season with ground Szechuan pepper, sprinkle with the sesame oil and serve immediately.

Dry Fried Shredded Beef

Dry frying is a unique Szechuan cooking method, in which the main ingredient is firstly stir-fried slowly over a low heat until dry, then finished off quickly with a mixture of other ingredients over a high heat.

INGREDIENTS

Serves 4

350–400g/12–14oz beef steak
1 large or 2 small carrots
2–3 sticks celery
30ml/2 tbsp sesame oil
15ml/1 tbsp Chinese rice wine or
  dry sherry
15ml/1 tbsp chilli bean sauce
15ml/1 tbsp light soy sauce
1 clove garlic, finely chopped
5ml/1 tsp light brown sugar
2–3 spring onions, finely chopped
2.5ml/½ tsp finely chopped fresh
  root ginger
ground Szechuan pepper

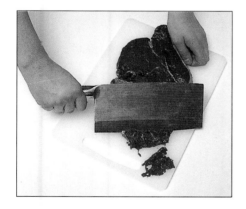

1 Cut the beef into matchstick-sized strips. Thinly shred the carrots and celery sticks.

2 Heat the sesame oil in a preheated wok (it will smoke very quickly). Reduce the heat and stir-fry the beef shreds with the rice wine or sherry until the colour changes.

3 Pour off the excess liquid and reserve. Continue stirring until the meat is absolutely dry.

4 Add the chilli bean sauce, soy sauce, garlic and sugar. Blend well, then add the carrot and celery shreds. Increase the heat to high and add the spring onions, ginger and the reserved liquid. Continue stirring, and when all the juice has evaporated, season with Szechuan pepper and serve.

Glazed Lamb

Lemon and honey make a classical stir-fry combination in sweet dishes, and this lamb recipe shows how well they work together in savoury dishes, too. Serve with a fresh mixed salad to complete this delicious dish.

Ingredients

Serves 4

450g/1lb boneless lean lamb
15ml/1 tbsp grapeseed oil
175g/6oz mangetouts, topped
  and tailed
3 spring onions, sliced
30ml/2 tbsp clear honey
juice of ½ lemon
30ml/2 tbsp chopped fresh coriander
15ml/1 tbsp sesame seeds
salt and ground black pepper

1 Using a cleaver, cut the lamb into thin strips.

Cook's Tip

This recipe would work just as well made with pork or chicken instead of lamb. You could substitute chopped fresh basil for the coriander if using chicken.

2 Heat the wok, then add the oil. When the oil is hot, stir-fry the lamb until browned all over. Remove from the wok and keep warm.

3 Add the mangetouts and spring onions to the hot wok and stir-fry for 30 seconds.

4 Return the lamb to the wok and add the honey, lemon juice, chopped coriander and sesame seeds and season well. Stir thoroughly to mix. Bring to the boil, then allow to bubble vigorously for 1 minute until the lamb is completely coated in the honey mixture. Serve immediately.

Minted Lamb Stir-fry

Lamb and mint have a long-established partnership that works particularly well in this full-flavoured stir-fry. Serve with plenty of crusty bread.

INGREDIENTS

Serves 2
275g/10oz lamb neck fillet
30ml/2 tbsp sunflower oil
10ml/2 tsp sesame oil
1 onion, roughly chopped
2 garlic cloves, crushed
1 fresh red chilli, seeded and
  finely chopped
75g/3oz fine green beans, halved
225g/8oz fresh spinach
30ml/2 tbsp oyster sauce
30ml/2 tbsp fish sauce
15ml/1 tbsp lemon juice
5ml/1 tsp caster sugar
45ml/3 tbsp chopped fresh mint
salt and ground black pepper
fresh mint sprigs, to garnish
crusty bread, to serve

1 Trim the lamb of any excess fat and cut into thin slices. Heat the sunflower and sesame oils in a preheated wok or large frying pan and stir-fry the lamb over a high heat until browned. Remove with a slotted spoon and drain on kitchen paper.

2 Add the onion, garlic and chilli to the wok and cook for 2–3 minutes. Add the beans to the wok and stir-fry for 3 minutes.

3 Stir in the spinach with the browned lamb, oyster sauce, fish sauce, lemon juice and sugar. Stir-fry for a further 3–4 minutes, or until the lamb is cooked through.

4 Sprinkle over the mint, adjust the seasoning and garnish with mint sprigs. Serve piping hot, with plenty of crusty bread to mop up all the juices.

good

Spicy Chicken Stir-fry

The chicken is marinated in an aromatic blend of spices and stir-fried with crisp vegetables. If you find it too spicy, serve with a spoonful of soured cream or yogurt. It's delicious hot or cold.

INGREDIENTS

Serves 4

2.5ml/½ tsp ground turmeric
2.5ml/½ tsp ground ginger
5ml/1 tsp salt
5ml/1 tsp ground black pepper
10ml/2 tsp ground cumin
15ml/1 tbsp ground coriander
15ml/1 tbsp caster sugar
450g/1lb boneless chicken breasts, skinned
1 bunch spring onions
4 celery sticks
2 red peppers, seeded
1 yellow pepper, seeded
175g/6oz courgettes
175g/6oz mangetouts or sugar snap peas
sunflower oil, for frying
15ml/1 tbsp lime juice
15ml/1 tbsp clear honey

1 Mix together the turmeric, ginger, salt, pepper, cumin, coriander and sugar in a bowl until well combined.

2 Cut the chicken into bite-sized strips. Add to the spice mixture and stir to coat the chicken pieces thoroughly. Set aside.

3 Prepare the vegetables. Cut the spring onions, celery and peppers into 5cm/2in-long, thin strips. Cut the courgettes at a slight angle into thin rounds and top and tail the mangetouts or sugar snap peas.

4 Heat 30ml/2 tbsp of oil in a preheated wok or large frying pan. Stir-fry the chicken in batches until cooked through and golden brown, adding a little more oil if necessary. Remove from the pan and keep warm.

5 Add a little more oil to the pan and cook the spring onions, celery, peppers and courgettes over a medium heat for about 8–10 minutes, until beginning to soften and turn golden. Add the mangetouts or sugar snap peas and cook for a further 2 minutes.

6 Return the chicken to the pan, with the lime juice and honey. Cook for 2 minutes. Serve immediately.

Shredded Chicken with Celery

The tender chicken breast contrasts with the crunchy texture of the celery, and the red chillies add colour and flavour.

INGREDIENTS

Serves 4
275g/10oz boneless chicken breast, skinned
5ml/1 tsp salt
½ egg white, lightly beaten
10ml/2 tsp cornflour paste
475ml/16fl oz/2 cups vegetable oil
1 celery heart, thinly shredded
1–2 fresh red chillies, seeded and thinly shredded
1 spring onion, thinly shredded
few strips of fresh root ginger, thinly shredded
5ml/1 tsp light brown sugar
15ml/1 tbsp Chinese rice wine or dry sherry
few drops of sesame oil

1 Using a sharp knife, thinly shred the chicken. In a bowl, mix together a pinch of the salt, the egg white and cornflour paste. Stir in the chicken.

2 Heat the oil in a preheated wok, add the chicken and stir to separate the shreds. When the chicken turns white, remove with a strainer and drain. Keep warm.

3 Pour off all but 30ml/2 tbsp of the oil. Add the celery, chillies, spring onion and ginger to the wok and stir-fry for 1 minute. Add the chicken, remaining salt, sugar and rice wine or dry sherry. Cook for 1 minute, then add the sesame oil. Serve hot.

Chicken with Chinese Vegetables

This dish makes an excellent family main course served with rice or noodles, but also combines with a selection of other dishes to serve as part of a dinner party menu.

INGREDIENTS

Serves 4
225–275g/8–10oz boneless chicken, skinned
5ml/1 tsp salt
½ egg white, lightly beaten
10ml/2 tsp cornflour paste
60ml/4 tbsp vegetable oil
6–8 small dried shiitake mushrooms, soaked in hot water
115g/4oz canned sliced bamboo shoots, drained

115g/4oz mangetouts
1 spring onion, cut into short sections
few small pieces of fresh root ginger
5ml/1 tsp light brown sugar
15ml/1 tbsp light soy sauce
15ml/1 tbsp Chinese rice wine or dry sherry
few drops of sesame oil

1 Cut the chicken into thin slices, each about the size of an oblong postage stamp. Place it in a bowl and mix with a pinch of the salt, the egg white and the cornflour paste.

2 Heat the oil in a preheated wok, add the chicken and stir-fry over medium heat for about 30 seconds, then remove with a slotted spoon and keep warm.

3 Add the vegetables to the wok and stir-fry over high heat for about 1 minute. Add the remaining salt, the sugar and chicken. Blend, then add the soy sauce and rice wine or dry sherry. Stir for a further 1 minute. Sprinkle with the sesame oil and serve.

Stir-fried Turkey with Broccoli and Mushrooms

This is a really easy, tasty supper dish which works well with chicken too.

INGREDIENTS

Serves 4

115g/4oz broccoli florets
4 spring onions
5ml/1 tsp cornflour
45ml/3 tbsp oyster sauce
15ml/1 tbsp dark soy sauce
120ml/4fl oz/$\frac{1}{2}$ cup chicken stock
10ml/2 tsp lemon juice
45ml/3 tbsp groundnut oil
450g/1lb turkey steaks cut into strips, about 5mm x 5cm/$\frac{1}{4}$ x 2in
1 small onion, chopped
2 garlic cloves, crushed
10ml/2 tsp grated fresh root ginger
115g/4oz fresh shiitake mushrooms, sliced
75g/3oz baby sweetcorn, halved lengthways
15ml/1 tbsp sesame oil
salt and ground black pepper
egg noodles, to serve

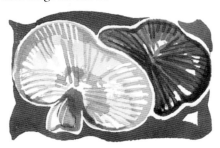

1 Divide the broccoli florets into smaller sprigs and cut the stalks into thin diagonal slices.

2 Finely chop the white parts of the spring onions and slice the green parts into thin shreds.

3 In a bowl, blend together the cornflour, oyster sauce, soy sauce, stock and lemon juice. Set aside.

4 Heat 30ml/2 tbsp of the groundnut oil in a preheated wok. Add the turkey and stir-fry for 2 minutes until golden and crisp at the edges. Remove from the wok and keep warm.

5 Add the remaining groundnut oil to the wok and stir-fry the chopped onion, garlic and ginger over a medium heat for about 1 minute. Increase the heat to high, add the broccoli, mushrooms and sweetcorn and stir-fry for 2 minutes.

6 Return the turkey to the wok, then add the sauce with the chopped spring onion and seasoning. Cook, stirring, for about 1 minute until the sauce has thickened. Stir in the sesame oil. Serve immediately on a bed of egg noodles with the finely shredded spring onion scattered on top.

COOK'S TIP

Cook fresh egg noodles in salted boiling water, stirring occasionally to prevent them from sticking. They are ready within a few minutes. Follow the packet instructions for cooking dried egg noodles.

VEGETABLES

Stir-fried Beansprouts

This is an easy way to cook up some tasty beansprouts in a wok. It is not necessary to top and tail them. Simply rinse in a bowl of cold water and discard any husks that float to the surface.

INGREDIENTS

Serves 4
2–3 spring onions
225g/8oz fresh beansprouts
45ml/3 tbsp vegetable oil
5ml/1 tsp salt
2.5ml/½ tsp light brown sugar
few drops sesame oil (optional)

1 Cut the spring onions into short sections about the same length as the beansprouts.

2 Heat the oil in a wok and stir-fry the beansprouts and spring onions for about 1 minute. Add the salt and sugar and continue stirring for 1 minute. Sprinkle with the sesame oil, if using, and serve. Do not overcook or the beansprouts will go soggy.

COOK'S TIP

Fresh and canned bean sprouts are readily available, but they can easily be grown at home for a constant and completely fresh supply. Scatter mung beans on several layers of damp kitchen paper on a small plate. Keep moist in a fairly warm place and the beans will sprout in a few days.

Stir-fried Spinach with Garlic and Sesame Seeds

The sesame seeds add a crunchy texture which contrasts well with the wilted spinach in this easy vegetable dish.

INGREDIENTS

Serves 2
225g/8oz fresh spinach, washed
25ml/1½ tbsp sesame seeds
30ml/2 tbsp groundnut oil
1.5ml/¼ tsp sea salt flakes
2–3 garlic cloves, sliced

—————— COOK'S TIP ——————

Take care when adding the spinach to the hot oil as it will spit furiously.

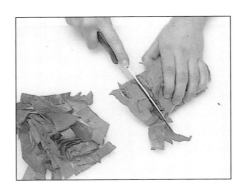

1 Shake the spinach to get rid of any excess water, then remove the stalks and discard any yellow or damaged leaves. Lay several spinach leaves one on top of another, roll up tightly and cut crossways into wide strips. Repeat with the remaining leaves.

2 Heat a wok to a medium heat, add the sesame seeds and dry fry, stirring constantly, for 1–2 minutes until golden brown. Transfer to a small bowl and set aside.

3 Add the oil to the wok and swirl it around. When hot, add the salt, spinach and garlic and stir-fry for 2 minutes until the spinach just wilts and the leaves are coated in oil.

4 Sprinkle over the dry-fried sesame seeds and toss well. Serve at once.

Chinese Leaves with Oyster Sauce

Here, Chinese leaves are prepared in a very simple way – stir-fried and served with oyster sauce. This Cantonese combination makes a simple, quickly prepared and tasty accompaniment to oriental or western seafood dishes. Vegetarians may prefer to substitute light soy or hoi-sin sauce for the oyster sauce used in this recipe.

INGREDIENTS

Serves 3–4
450g/1lb Chinese leaves
30ml/2 tbsp groundnut oil
15–30ml/1–2 tbsp oyster sauce

1 Trim the Chinese leaves, removing any discoloured leaves and damaged stems. Tear into manageable pieces.

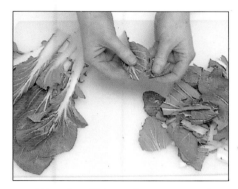

2 Heat a wok until hot, add the oil and swirl it around.

3 Add the Chinese leaves and stir-fry for 2–3 minutes until they have wilted a little.

4 Add the oyster sauce and continue to stir-fry for a few seconds more until the leaves are cooked but still slightly crisp. Serve immediately.

COOK'S TIP

You can replace the Chinese leaves with Chinese flowering cabbage, which is also known by its Cantonese name *choi sam*. It has bright green leaves and tiny yellow flowers, which are also eaten along with the leaves and stalks. It is available from oriental supermarkets.

Black Bean and Vegetable Stir-fry

The secret of a quick stir-fry is proper preparation of all the ingredients first. It is important that the ingredients are added to the wok in the right order so that the larger or thicker pieces have a longer cooking time than the smaller pieces – even if this is a difference of only a few millimetres and a few seconds!

INGREDIENTS

Serves 4

8 spring onions
225g/8oz button mushrooms
1 red pepper
1 green pepper
2 large carrots
60ml/4 tbsp sesame oil
2 garlic cloves, crushed
60ml/4 tbsp black bean sauce
90ml/6 tbsp warm water
225g/8oz beansprouts
salt and ground black pepper

1 Thinly slice the spring onions and button mushrooms.

2 Cut both the peppers in half, remove the seeds and slice the flesh into thin strips.

3 Cut the carrots in half. Cut each half into thin strips lengthways. Stack the slices and cut through them to make very fine strips.

4 Heat the oil in a large preheated wok until very hot. Add the spring onions and garlic and stir-fry for 30 seconds.

5 Add the mushrooms, peppers and carrots. Stir-fry for 5–6 minutes over a high heat until the vegetables are just beginning to soften.

6 Mix the black bean sauce with the water. Add to the wok and cook for 3–4 minutes. Stir in the beansprouts and cook for 1 minute more, until all the vegetables are coated in the sauce. Season to taste, then serve at once.

--- COOK'S TIP ---

Black bean sauce is made from salted black beans – which have a very distinctive flavour – that have been crushed and mixed with a variety of spices, such as ginger and chilli. It is quite a thick paste and readily available in jars, bottles and cans from large supermarkets and oriental food stores. Store in the refrigerator after opening.

Stir-fried Chinese Leaves with Mushrooms

You can stir-fry fresh button mushrooms in this recipe, if you prefer them or if fresh or canned straw mushrooms are not available.

INGREDIENTS

Serves 4
225g/8oz fresh straw mushrooms or
   350g/12oz can straw
   mushrooms, drained
60ml/4 tbsp vegetable oil
400g/14oz Chinese leaves, cut
   in strips
5ml/1 tsp salt
5ml/1 tsp light brown sugar
15ml/1tbsp cornflour paste
120ml/4fl oz/½ cup milk

1 Cut the mushrooms in half lengthways. Heat half the oil, stir-fry the Chinese leaves for 2 minutes, then add half the salt and half the sugar. Stir for 1 minute.

2 Transfer the Chinese leaves to a warm serving dish. Add the mushrooms to the wok and stir-fry for 1 minute. Add the remaining salt and sugar, cook for 1 minute, then thicken with the cornflour paste and milk. Serve with the Chinese leaves.

---— COOK'S TIP —---

The Chinese approach cooking with the same overall desire for harmony and balance that characterizes their ancient philosophy. Recipes for stir-fried vegetables are not simply an arbitrary combination of whatever is to hand — they should balance and complement each other in both colour and texture. The delicious slipperiness of straw mushrooms complements the crunchier texture of the Chinese leaves, so it is best to use them if at all possible. Canned straw mushrooms are available from oriental food stores. Do not overcook or the harmony and balance will be lost.

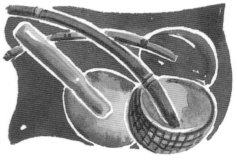

Chinese Vegetable Stir-fry

This is a typical stir-fried vegetable dish popular all over China. Chinese leaves are like a cross between a cabbage and a crunchy lettuce, with a delicious peppery flavour.

INGREDIENTS

Serves 4
45ml/3 tbsp sunflower oil
15ml/1 tbsp sesame oil
1 garlic clove, chopped
225g/8oz broccoli florets, cut into small pieces
115g/4oz sugar snap peas
1 head Chinese leaves, about 450g/1lb, or Savoy cabbage, sliced
4 spring onions, finely chopped
30ml/2 tbsp soy sauce
30ml/2 tbsp Chinese rice wine or dry sherry
30–45ml/2–3 tbsp water
15ml/1 tbsp sesame seeds, lightly toasted

1 Heat the sunflower and sesame oils in a preheated wok or large frying pan, add the garlic and stir-fry for 30 seconds.

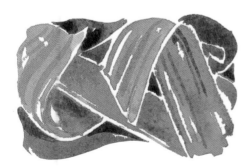

2 Add the broccoli florets and stir-fry for 3 minutes. Add the sugar snap peas and cook for 2 minutes, then toss in the Chinese leaves or cabbage and the spring onions and stir-fry for a further 2 minutes.

3 Pour on the soy sauce, rice wine or dry sherry and water and stir-fry for a further 4 minutes, or until the vegetables are just tender. Sprinkle with the toasted sesame seeds and serve hot.

Chinese Garlic Mushrooms

Tofu is high in protein and very low in fat, so it is an extremely useful and healthy food to keep handy for quick meals and snacks like this one.

Ingredients

Serves 4
8 large open mushrooms
3 spring onions, sliced
1 garlic clove, crushed
30ml/2 tbsp oyster sauce
275g/10oz marinated tofu, cut into small dice
200g/7oz can sweetcorn kernels, drained
10ml/2 tsp sesame oil
salt and ground black pepper

1 Finely chop the mushroom stalks and mix with the spring onions, garlic and oyster sauce.

2 Stir in the diced, marinated tofu and sweetcorn, season well with salt and pepper, then spoon the filling into the mushrooms.

3 Brush the edges of the mushrooms with the sesame oil. Arrange the stuffed mushrooms in a baking dish and bake in a preheated oven at 200°C/400°F/Gas 6 for 12–15 minutes, until the mushrooms are just tender, then serve at once.

--- Cook's Tip ---

If you prefer, omit the oyster sauce and use light soy sauce instead.

Stir-fried Mixed Vegetables

When selecting different items for a stir-fried dish, never mix the ingredients indiscriminately. The idea is to achieve a harmonious balance of colour and texture.

INGREDIENTS

Serves 4
225g/8oz Chinese leaves
115g/4oz baby corn cobs
115g/4oz broccoli
1 medium or 2 small carrots
60ml/4 tbsp vegetable oil
5ml/1 tsp salt
5ml/1 tsp light brown sugar
vegetable stock or water, if necessary
15ml/1 tbsp light soy sauce
few drops of sesame oil (optional)

2 Heat the oil in a preheated wok and stir-fry the vegetables for about 2 minutes.

3 Add the salt and sugar and a little stock or water, if necessary, and continue stirring for another minute. Add the soy sauce and sesame oil, if using. Blend well and serve.

1 Cut the vegetables into roughly similar shapes and sizes.

NOODLES
& RICE

Noodles with Chicken, Prawns and Ham

Egg noodles can be cooked up to 24 hours in advance and kept in a bowl of cold water.

INGREDIENTS

Serves 4–6

275g/10oz dried egg noodles
15ml/1 tbsp vegetable oil
1 medium onion, chopped
1 garlic clove, crushed
2.5cm/1in fresh root ginger, chopped
50g/2oz canned water chestnuts, drained and sliced
15ml/1 tbsp light soy sauce
30ml/2 tbsp fish sauce or strong chicken stock
175g/6oz cooked chicken breast, sliced
150g/5oz cooked ham, thickly sliced and cut into short fingers
225g/8oz cooked prawn tails, peeled
175g/6oz beansprouts
200g/7oz canned baby corn cobs, drained
2 limes, cut into wedges, and 1 small bunch coriander, shredded, to garnish

1 Cook the noodles according to the packet instructions. Drain well and set aside.

2 Heat the oil in a preheated wok or frying pan. Fry the onion, garlic and ginger for 3 minutes, or until soft but not coloured. Add the chestnuts, soy sauce, fish sauce or chicken stock, chicken breast, ham and prawns.

3 Add the noodles, beansprouts and baby corn cobs and stir-fry for 6–8 minutes, until heated through. Transfer to a warmed serving dish, garnish with the lime wedges and shredded coriander and serve immediately.

Soft Fried Noodles

This is a very basic dish for serving as an accompaniment or for those occasions when you are feeling a little peckish and fancy something simple. Break an egg into the noodles if you want to add protein. They are also good tossed with oyster sauce and a dollop of chilli black bean sauce.

INGREDIENTS

Serves 4–6
350g/12oz dried egg noodles
30ml/2 tbsp vegetable oil
30ml/2 tbsp finely chopped
   spring onions
soy sauce, to taste
salt and freshly ground black pepper

1 Cook the noodles in a large saucepan of boiling water until just tender, following the directions on the packet. Drain, rinse under cold running water and drain again thoroughly.

2 Heat the oil in a wok and swirl it around. Add the spring onions and fry for 30 seconds. Add the noodles, stirring gently to separate the strands.

3 Reduce the heat and fry the noodles until they are heated through, lightly browned and crisp on the outside, but still soft inside.

4 Season with soy sauce, salt and pepper. Serve at once.

Egg Fried Noodles

Yellow bean sauce gives these noodles a savoury flavour.

INGREDIENTS

Serves 4–6
350g/12oz medium-thick egg noodles
60ml/4 tbsp vegetable oil
4 spring onions, cut into
   1 cm/½ in rounds
juice of 1 lime
15ml/1 tbsp soy sauce
2 garlic cloves, finely chopped
175g/6oz skinless, boneless chicken
   breast, sliced
175g/6oz raw prawns, peeled
   and deveined
175g/6oz squid, cleaned and cut into
   rings
15ml/1 tbsp yellow bean sauce
15ml/1 tbsp fish sauce
15ml/1 tbsp soft light brown sugar
2 eggs
coriander leaves, to garnish

1 Cook the noodles in a saucepan of boiling water until just tender, then drain well and set aside.

2 Heat half the oil in a wok or large frying pan. Add the spring onions, stir-fry for 2 minutes, then add the noodles, lime juice and soy sauce and stir-fry for 2–3 minutes. Transfer the mixture to a bowl and keep warm.

3 Heat the remaining oil in the wok or pan. Add the garlic, chicken, prawns and squid. Stir-fry over a high heat until cooked.

4 Stir in the yellow bean paste, fish sauce and sugar, then break the eggs into the mixture, stirring gently until they set.

5 Add the noodles, toss lightly to mix, and heat through. Serve garnished with coriander leaves.

Noodles with Ginger and Coriander

Here is a simple noodle dish that goes well with most oriental dishes. It can also be served as a snack for two or three people.

INGREDIENTS

Serves 4–6
handful fresh coriander sprigs
225g/8oz dried egg noodles
45ml/3 tbsp groundnut oil
5cm/2in fresh root ginger,
   finely shredded
6–8 spring onions, shredded
30ml/2 tbsp light soy sauce
salt and ground black pepper

COOK'S TIP

Many of the dried egg noodles available are sold packed in layers. As a guide, allow 1 layer of noodles per person as an average portion for a main dish.

1 Strip the leaves from the coriander sprigs. Pile them on a chopping board and chop them roughly, using a cleaver or large sharp knife.

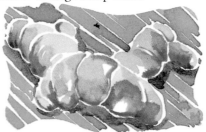

2 Cook the noodles according to the packet instructions. Rinse under cold water and drain well. Toss them in 15ml/1 tbsp of the oil.

3 Heat a wok until hot, add the remaining oil and swirl it around. Add the ginger and stir-fry for a few seconds, then add the noodles and spring onions. Stir-fry for 3–4 minutes until hot.

4 Sprinkle over the soy sauce, coriander and seasoning. Toss well, then serve at once.

Fried Noodles with Beansprouts and Asparagus

Soft fried noodles contrast beautifully with crisp beansprouts and asparagus.

INGREDIENTS
Serves 4

115g/4oz dried egg noodles
60ml/4 tbsp vegetable oil
1 small onion, chopped
2.5cm/1in fresh root ginger, peeled
   and grated
2 garlic cloves, crushed
175g/6oz young asparagus
   spears, trimmed
115g/4oz beansprouts
4 spring onions, sliced
45ml/3 tbsp soy sauce
salt and ground black pepper

1 Bring a pan of salted water to the boil. Add the noodles and cook for 2–3 minutes, until tender. Drain and toss them in 30ml/2 tbsp of the oil.

2 Heat the remaining oil in a preheated wok until very hot. Add the onion, ginger and garlic and stir-fry for 2–3 minutes. Add the asparagus and stir-fry for a further 2–3 minutes.

3 Add the noodles and beansprouts and stir-fry for 2 minutes.

4 Stir in the spring onions and soy sauce. Season to taste, adding salt sparingly as the soy sauce will add quite a salty flavour. Stir-fry for 1 minute, then serve at once.

Spicy Szechuan Noodles

INGREDIENTS

Serves 4
350g/12oz thick noodles
175g/6oz cooked chicken,
    shredded
50g/2oz roasted cashew nuts

For the dressing
4 spring onions, chopped
30ml/2 tbsp chopped coriander
2 garlic cloves, chopped
30ml/2 tbsp smooth peanut butter
30ml/2 tbsp sweet chilli sauce
15ml/1 tbsp soy sauce
15ml/1 tbsp sherry vinegar
15ml/1 tbsp sesame oil
30ml/2 tbsp olive oil
30ml/2 tbsp chicken stock
    or water
10 toasted Szechuan peppercorns,
    ground

1 Cook the noodles in a saucepan of boiling water until just tender, following the directions on the packet. Drain, rinse under cold running water and drain well.

2 While the noodles are cooking combine all the ingredients for the dressing in a large bowl and whisk together well.

3 Add the noodles, shredded chicken and cashew nuts to the dressing, toss gently to coat and adjust the seasoning to taste. Serve at once.

> ——— COOK'S TIP ———
>
> You could substitute cooked turkey or pork for the chicken for a change.

Sesame Noodles with Spring Onions

This simple but very tasty warm salad can be prepared and cooked in just a few minutes.

INGREDIENTS

Serves 4
2 garlic cloves, roughly chopped
30ml/2 tbsp Chinese sesame paste
15ml/1 tbsp dark sesame oil
30ml/2 tbsp soy sauce
30ml/2 tbsp rice wine
15ml/1 tbsp honey
pinch of five-spice powder
350g/12oz soba or
    buckwheat noodles
4 spring onions, finely
    sliced diagonally
50g/2oz beansprouts
7.5cm/3in piece of cucumber, cut
    into matchsticks
toasted sesame seeds
salt and freshly ground black pepper

1 Process the garlic, sesame paste, oil, soy sauce, rice wine, honey and five-spice powder with a pinch each of salt and pepper in a blender or food processor until smooth.

2 Cook the noodles in a saucepan of boiling water until just tender, following the directions on the packet. Drain the noodles immediately and tip them into a bowl.

3 Toss the hot noodles with the dressing and the spring onions. Top with the beansprouts, cucumber and sesame seeds and serve.

> ——— COOK'S TIP ———
>
> If you can't find Chinese sesame paste, then use either tahini paste or smooth peanut butter instead.

Rice Noodles with Beef and Black Bean Sauce

This is an excellent combination – beef with a chilli sauce tossed with silky smooth rice noodles.

INGREDIENTS

Serves 4

450g/1lb fresh rice noodles
60ml/4 tbsp vegetable oil
1 onion, finely sliced
2 garlic cloves, finely chopped
2 slices fresh root ginger,
    finely chopped
225g/8oz mixed peppers, seeded and
    cut into strips
350g/12oz rump steak, finely sliced
    against the grain
45ml/3 tbsp fermented black beans,
    rinsed in warm water, drained
    and chopped
30ml/2 tbsp soy sauce
30ml/2 tbsp oyster sauce
15ml/1 tbsp chilli black bean sauce
15ml/1 tbsp cornflour
120ml/4fl oz/½ cup stock or water
2 spring onions, finely chopped, and
    2 red chillies, seeded and finely
    sliced, to garnish

1 Rinse the noodles under hot water; drain well. Heat half the oil in a wok or large frying pan, swirling it around. Add the onion, garlic, ginger and mixed pepper strips. Stir-fry for 3–5 minutes, then remove with a slotted spoon and keep hot.

2 Add the remaining oil to the wok. When hot, add the sliced beef and fermented black beans and stir-fry over a high heat for 5 minutes or until they are cooked.

3 In a small bowl, blend the soy sauce, oyster sauce and chilli black bean sauce with the cornflour and stock or water until smooth. Add the mixture to the wok, then return the onion mixture to the wok and cook, stirring, for 1 minute.

4 Add the noodles and mix lightly. Stir over a medium heat until the noodles are heated through. Adjust the seasoning if necessary. Serve at once, garnished with the chopped spring onions and chillies.

Special Chow Mein

Lap cheong is a special air-dried Chinese sausage. It is available from most Chinese supermarkets. If you cannot buy it, substitute with either diced ham, chorizo or salami.

INGREDIENTS

Serves 4–6

45ml/3 tbsp vegetable oil
2 garlic cloves, sliced
5ml/1 tsp chopped fresh root ginger
2 red chillies, chopped
2 lap cheong, about 75g/3oz, rinsed
 and sliced (optional)
1 boneless chicken breast, thinly sliced
16 uncooked tiger prawns, peeled, tails
 left intact, and deveined
115g/4oz green beans
225g/8oz beansprouts
50g/2oz garlic chives
450g/1lb egg noodles, cooked in
 boiling water until tender
30ml/2 tbsp soy sauce
15ml/1 tbsp oyster sauce
salt and freshly ground black pepper
15ml/1 tbsp sesame oil
2 spring onions, shredded, to garnish
15ml/1 tbsp coriander leaves,
 to garnish

1 Heat 15ml/1 tbsp of the oil in a wok or large frying pan and fry the garlic, ginger and chillies. Add the lap cheong, chicken, prawns and beans. Stir-fry for about 2 minutes over a high heat or until the chicken and prawns are cooked. Transfer the mixture to a bowl and set aside.

2 Heat the rest of the oil in the same wok. Add the beansprouts and garlic chives. Stir fry for 1–2 minutes.

3 Add the noodles and toss and stir to mix. Season with soy sauce, oyster sauce, salt and pepper.

4 Return the prawn mixture to the wok. Reheat and mix well with the noodles. Stir in the sesame oil. Serve garnished with spring onions and coriander leaves.

Crispy Noodles with Mixed Vegetables

In this dish, rice vermicelli noodles are deep fried until crisp, then tossed into a colourful selection of stir-fried vegetables.

INGREDIENTS

Serves 4

2 large carrots
2 courgettes
4 spring onions
115g/4oz yard-long beans or
    green beans
115g/4oz dried vermicelli rice noodles
    or cellophane noodles
groundnut oil, for deep frying
2.5cm/1in fresh root ginger, shredded
1 fresh red chilli, sliced
115g/4oz fresh shiitake or button
    mushrooms, thickly sliced
few Chinese cabbage leaves,
    roughly shredded
75g/3oz beansprouts
30ml/2 tbsp light soy sauce
30ml/2 tbsp Chinese rice wine or
    dry sherry
5ml/1 tsp sugar
30ml/2 tbsp roughly torn fresh
    coriander leaves

— COOK'S TIP —

Vermicelli rice noodles, which are thin and brittle, look like a bundle of white hair. They cook almost instantly in hot liquid, provided they have first been soaked in warm water. Rice noodles can also be deep fried. Cellophane noodles, which are made from ground mung beans, look a little like bundles of candy floss. They are opaque white when dried and expand and become translucent after soaking. Cellophane noodles are also known as bean thread, transparent and glass noodles. Dried noodles must be soaked for 5 minutes in hot water before cooking.

1 Cut the carrots and courgettes into fine sticks. Shred the spring onions into similar-sized pieces. Trim the beans and cut them into short lengths.

2 Break the noodles into lengths of about 7.5cm/3in. Half-fill a wok with oil and heat it to 180°C/350°F. Deep fry the raw noodles, a handful at a time, for 1–2 minutes until puffed and crispy. Drain on kitchen paper. Pour off all but 30ml/2 tbsp of the oil.

3 Reheat the oil in the wok. When hot, add the beans and stir-fry for 2–3 minutes.

4 Add the ginger, red chilli, mushrooms, carrots and courgettes and stir-fry for 1–2 minutes. Add the Chinese cabbage, beansprouts and spring onions. Stir-fry for 1 minute, then add the soy sauce, rice wine or sherry and sugar. Cook, stirring, for about 30 seconds.

5 Add the noodles and coriander and toss to mix, taking care not to crush the noodles too much. Serve at once, piled up on a plate.

Plain Rice

Use long-grain or patna rice or fragrant rice from Thailand. Allow 50g/2oz raw rice per person. If you use fragrant Thai rice, omit the salt.

INGREDIENTS

Serves 4
225g/8oz/generous 1 cup rice
about 250ml/8fl oz/1 cup water
pinch of salt
2.5ml/½ tsp vegetable oil

1 Wash and rinse the rice. Place the rice in a saucepan and add the water. There should be no more than 2cm/¾in of water above the surface of the rice.

2 Bring to the boil, add the salt and oil, then stir to prevent the rice sticking to the bottom of the pan. Reduce the heat to very, very low, cover and cook for 15–20 minutes.

3 Remove from the heat and leave to stand, still covered, for 10 minutes. Fluff up the rice with a fork or spoon just before serving.

Egg-fried Rice

Use rice with a fairly firm texture. Ideally, the raw rice should be soaked in water for a short time before cooking.

INGREDIENTS

Serves 4
3 eggs
5ml/1 tsp salt
30–45ml/2–3 tbsp vegetable oil
450g/1lb cooked rice
2 spring onions, finely chopped
115g/4oz frozen peas

1 In a bowl, lightly beat the eggs with a pinch of the salt and a few pieces of the spring onions.

2 Heat the oil in a preheated wok, and lightly scramble the eggs.

3 Add the cooked rice and stir to make sure that each grain of rice is separated. Add the remaining salt, spring onions and the peas. Blend well, allow to heat through and serve.

Egg Foo Yung

A great way of turning a bowl of leftover cooked rice into a meal for four, this dish is tasty and full of texture.

INGREDIENTS

Serves 4
3 eggs, beaten
pinch of Chinese five-spice
   powder (optional)
45ml/3 tbsp groundnut or
   sunflower oil
4 spring onions, sliced
1 garlic clove, crushed
1 small green pepper, seeded and
   chopped
115g/4oz beansprouts
225g/8oz/generous 1 cup white
   rice, cooked
45ml/3 tbsp light soy sauce
15ml/1 tbsp sesame oil
salt and ground black pepper

1 Season the eggs with salt and pepper to taste and beat in the five-spice powder, if using.

2 Heat 15ml/1 tbsp of the oil in a preheated wok or large frying pan and, when quite hot, pour in the egg. Cook rather like an omelette, pulling the mixture away from the sides and allowing the rest to slip underneath.

3 Cook the egg until firm, then tip out. Chop the omelette into small strips and set aside.

4 Heat the remaining oil and stir-fry the onions, garlic, green pepper and beansprouts for about 2 minutes, stirring and tossing continuously.

5 Mix in the cooked rice and heat thoroughly, stirring well. Add the soy sauce and sesame oil, then return the egg strips and mix in well. Serve immediately, piping hot.

Special Fried Rice

Special fried rice is so substantial and tasty that it is another rice dish that is almost a meal in itself.

INGREDIENTS

Serves 4
50g/2oz peeled, cooked prawns
50g/2oz cooked ham
115g/4oz green peas
3 eggs
5ml/1 tsp salt
2 spring onions, finely chopped
60ml/4 tbsp vegetable oil
15ml/1 tbsp light soy sauce
15ml/1 tbsp Chinese rice wine or
 dry sherry
450g/1lb cooked rice

1 Pat dry the prawns with kitchen paper. Cut the ham into small dice about the same size as the peas.

2 In a bowl, lightly beat the eggs with a pinch of the salt and a few pieces of the spring onions.

3 Heat about half of the oil in a preheated wok, stir-fry the peas, prawns and ham for 1 minute, then add the soy sauce and rice wine or sherry. Remove and keep warm.

4 Heat the remaining oil in the wok and lightly scramble the eggs. Add the rice and stir to make sure that each grain of rice is separated. Add the remaining salt, spring onions and the prawns, ham and peas. Blend well and serve either hot or cold.

  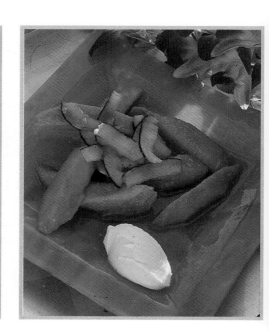

DESSERTS

Date and Walnut Crisps

Try this sweet version of fried wontons; they make a truly scrumptious snack or dessert.

INGREDIENTS

Makes 15
25–30 dried dates, stoned
50g/2oz/½ cup walnuts
30ml/2 tbsp light brown sugar
pinch of ground cinnamon
30 wonton wrappers
1 egg, beaten
oil, for deep-frying
fresh mint sprigs, to decorate
icing sugar, for dusting

1 Chop the dates and walnuts roughly. Place them in a bowl and add the sugar and cinnamon. Mix well.

2 Lay a wonton wrapper on a flat surface. Centre a spoonful of the filling on the wrapper, brush the edges with beaten egg and cover with a second wrapper. Lightly press the edges together to seal. Make more filled wontons in the same way.

3 Heat the oil to 180°C/350°F in a wok or deep-fryer. Deep-fry the wontons, a few at a time, until golden. Do not crowd the pan. Remove them with a slotted spoon and drain on kitchen paper. Serve warm, decorated with mint and dusted with icing sugar.

Apples and Raspberries in Rose Pouchong Syrup

This delightfully fragrant and quick-to-prepare Asian dessert couples the subtle flavours of apples and raspberries, both of which belong to the rose family, within an infusion of rose-scented tea.

INGREDIENTS

Serves 4
5ml/1 tsp rose pouchong tea
5ml/1 tsp rose water (optional)
50g/2oz/¼ cup sugar
5ml/1 tsp lemon juice
5 dessert apples
175g/6oz/1½ cups fresh raspberries

1 Warm a large tea pot. Add the rose pouchong tea and 900ml/1½ pints/ 3¾ cups of boiling water together with the rose water, if using. Allow to stand and infuse for 4 minutes.

2 Measure the sugar and lemon juice into a stainless steel saucepan. Strain in the tea and stir to dissolve the sugar.

3 Peel and core the apples, then cut into quarters.

4 Poach the apples in the syrup for about 5 minutes.

5 Transfer the apples and syrup to a large metal tray and leave to cool to room temperature.

6 Pour the cooled apples and syrup into a bowl, add the raspberries and mix to combine. Spoon into individual dishes or bowls and serve immediately.

Toffee Apples

A variety of fruits, such as bananas and pineapple, can be prepared and cooked in this way.

INGREDIENTS

Serves 4

4 firm eating apples
115g/4oz plain flour
about 120ml/4fl oz/½ cup water
1 egg, beaten
vegetable oil, for deep frying, plus
   30ml/2 tbsp for the toffee
115g/4oz sugar

1 Peel and core each apple and cut into eight pieces. Dust each piece of apple with a little of the flour.

2 Sift the remaining flour into a mixing bowl, then slowly add the cold water and stir well to make a smooth batter. Add the beaten egg and blend well.

3 Heat the oil for deep frying in a wok. Dip the apple pieces in the batter and deep fry for about 3 minutes or until golden. Remove and drain. Drain off the oil.

4 Heat the remaining oil in the wok, add the sugar and stir continuously until the sugar has caramelized. Quickly add the apple pieces and blend well so that each piece of apple is thoroughly coated with the toffee. Dip the apple pieces in cold water to harden before serving.

Mango and Coconut Stir-fry

Choose a ripe mango for this recipe. If you buy one that is a little under-ripe, leave it in a warm place for a day or two before using.

INGREDIENTS

Serves 4
¼ coconut
1 large, ripe mango
juice of 2 limes
rind of 2 limes, finely grated
15ml/1 tbsp sunflower oil
15g/½ oz butter
30ml/2 tbsp clear honey
crème fraîche, to serve

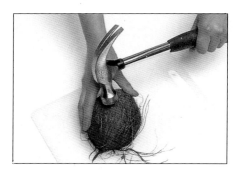

1 Prepare the coconut flakes by draining the milk from the coconut and peeling the flesh with a vegetable peeler.

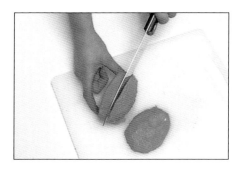

2 Peel the mango. Cut the stone out of the middle of the fruit. Cut each half of the mango into slices.

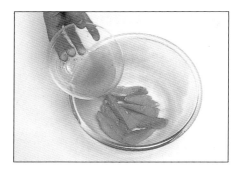

3 Place the mango slices in a bowl and pour over the lime juice and rind, to marinate them.

4 Meanwhile heat a wok, then add 10ml/2 tsp of the oil. When the oil is hot, add the butter. When the butter has melted, stir in the coconut flakes and stir-fry for 1–2 minutes until the coconut is golden brown. Remove and drain on kitchen paper. Wipe out the wok. Strain the mango slices, reserving the juice.

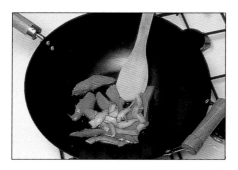

5 Heat the wok and add the remaining oil. When the oil is hot, add the mango and stir-fry for 1–2 minutes, then add the juice and allow to bubble and reduce for 1 minute. Stir in the honey, sprinkle on the coconut flakes and serve with crème fraîche.

--- COOK'S TIP ---

You can sometimes buy "fresh" coconut that has already been cracked open and is sold in pieces ready for use from supermarkets, but buying the whole nut ensures greater freshness. Choose one that is heavy for its size and shake it so that you can hear the milk sloshing about. A "dry" coconut will almost certainly have rancid flesh. You can simply crack the shell with a hammer, preferably with the nut inside a plastic bag, but it may be better to pierce the two ends with a sharp nail or skewer first in order to collect and save the coconut milk. An alternative method is to drain the milk first and then heat the nut briefly in the oven until it cracks. Whichever method you choose, it is then fairly easy to extract the flesh and chop or shave it.

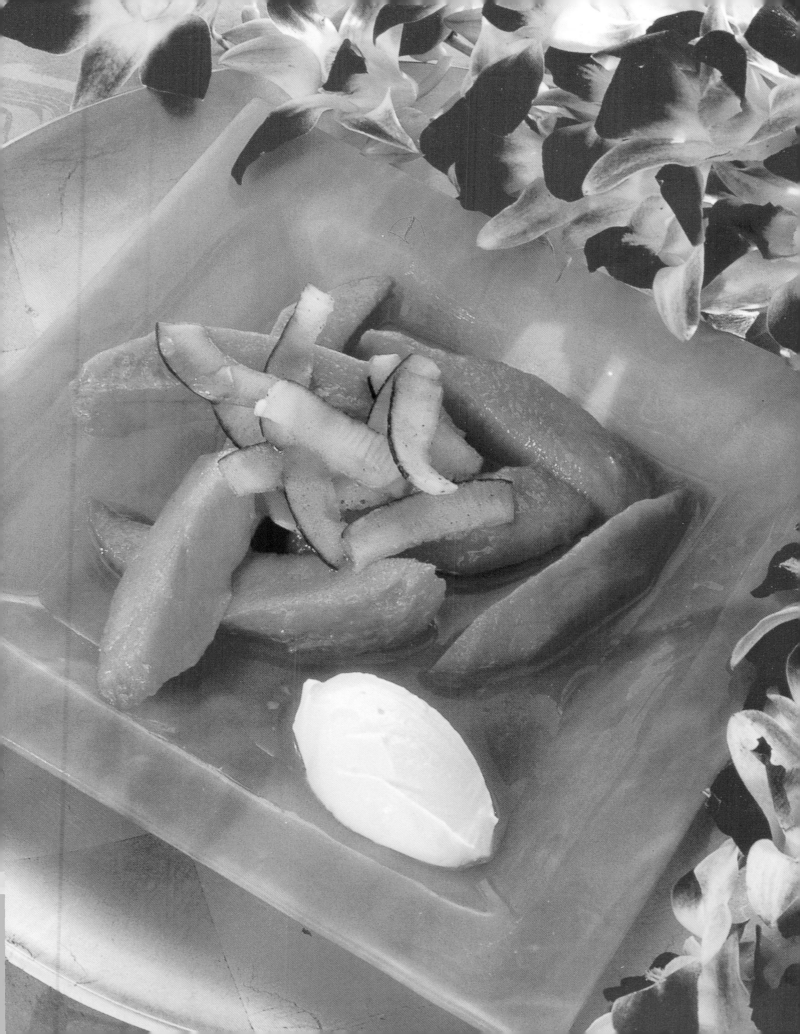

Wonton Twists

These little twists are perfect when you want a quick snack.

INGREDIENTS

Makes 24
12 wonton wrappers
1 egg, beaten
15ml/1 tbsp black sesame seeds
oil for deep frying
icing sugar for dusting (optional)

1 Cut the wonton wrappers in half and make a lengthways slit in the centre of each piece with a sharp knife.

2 Take one wonton at a time and pull one end through the slit, stretching it a little as you go.

3 Brush each twist with a little beaten egg. Dip the wonton twists briefly in black sesame seeds to coat them lightly.

4 Heat the oil in a deep fryer or large saucepan to 190°C/375°F. Add a few wonton twists at a time so they do not overcrowd the pan. Fry for about 1–2 minutes on each side until crisp and light golden brown. Remove each twist and drain on kitchen paper. Dust the wonton twists with icing sugar, if you like, and serve at once.

— COOK'S TIP —

Use ordinary sesame seeds in place of the black ones if you prefer.

Fried Wontons and Ice Cream

Americans have their cookies and ice cream – here is the Chinese equivalent. Serve it with fresh or poached fruits or fruit sauces for an impressive treat.

INGREDIENTS

Serves 4
oil for deep frying
12 wonton wrappers
8 scoops of your favourite
  ice cream

— COOK'S TIP —

Try using two flavours of ice cream – chocolate and strawberry perhaps, or vanilla and coffee. For a sophisticated adults-only treat, drizzle over a spoonful of your favourite liqueur.

1 Heat the oil in a deep fryer or large saucepan to 190°C/375°F.

2 Add a few wonton wrappers at a time so that they do not crowd the pan too much. Fry for 1–2 minutes on each side until the wrappers are crisp and light golden brown.

3 Leave the cooked wontons to drain on kitchen paper.

4 To serve, place one wonton on each plate. Place a scoop of ice cream on top of each wonton. Top with a second wonton, then add another ball of ice cream and finish with a final wonton. Serve at once.

INDEX